T0419629

CHINA IN THE 21ST CENTURY

THE CHINESE ECONOMY

CHINA IN THE 21ST CENTURY

Additional books in this series can be found on Nova's website at:

https://www.novapublishers.com/catalog/index.php?cPath=23_29&seriesp=China+in+the+21st+Century

Additional E-books in this series can be found on Nova's website at:

https://www.novapublishers.com/catalog/index.php?cPath=23_29&seriespe=China+in+the+21st+Century

CHINA IN THE 21ST CENTURY

THE CHINESE ECONOMY

BENJAMIN A. TYLER
EDITOR

Nova Science Publishers, Inc.
New York

For permission to use material from this book please contact us:
Telephone 631-231-7269; Fax 631-231-8175
Web Site: http://www.novapublishers.com

LIBRARY OF CONGRESS CATALOGING-IN-PUBLICATION DATA

Available upon request

ISBN : 978-1-60876-937-7

Published by Nova Science Publishers, Inc. ✢ New York

CONTENTS

PREFACE

Since the initiation of economic reforms 30 years ago, China has become one of the world's fastest-growing economies. However, the current global economic crisis has hit China hard - real GDP growth slowed to 9% in 2008, and many analysts predict the economy will slow even more sharply in 2009. This is of great concern to the Chinese government, which views healthy economic growth as critical to maintaining social stability. China also faces a number of other challenges to its economic growth and stability, including pervasive government corruption, an inefficient banking system, over-dependence on exports and fixed investment for growth, the lack of rule of law, severe pollution, and widening income disparities. This new book describes in detail the despairing economic conditions that are affecting China and the steps that need to be taken in order correct these issues.

Chapter 1 - Although the Chinese economy is booming, the People's Republic of China (PRC) faces five major challenges to sustain rapid economic growth in the future:

- unfavorable demographics;
- corruption and a weak rule of law;
- financially distressed state-owned enterprises and state-influenced enterprises;
- a dysfunctional financial system; and
- domestic and international imbalances.

The PRC's response to these challenges will, of course, determine the future performance of the Chinese economy. However, since the Chinese economy is so large and well integrated into the global economy, the performance of the Chinese economy will also affect the performance of the United States and other economies in the world.

So far, the PRC's approach to reform has been incremental. This incremental approach may be reaching the limits of its effectiveness. The challenges that the PRC now confronts are deeply interrelated. A more comprehensive approach to reform is needed.

Chapter 2 - Many Members of Congress charge that China's policy of accumulating foreign reserves (especially U.S. dollars) to influence the value of its currency constitutes a form of currency manipulation intended to make its exports cheaper and imports into China more expensive than they would be under free market conditions. They further contend that this policy has caused a surge in the U.S. trade deficit with China in recent years and has been a major factor in the loss of U.S. manufacturing jobs. Although China made modest reforms to its currency policy in 2005, resulting in a gradual appreciation of its currency (about 19% through June 3, 2009), many Members contend the reforms have not gone far enough and have warned of potential punitive legislative action. Although an undervalued Chinese currency has likely hurt some sectors of the U.S. economy, it has benefited others. For example, U.S. consumers have gained from the supply of low-cost Chinese goods (which helps to control inflation), as have U.S. firms using Chinesemade parts and materials (which helps such firms become more globally competitive). In addition, China has used its abundant foreign exchange reserves to buy U.S. securities, including U.S. Treasury securities, which are used to help fund the Federal budget deficit. Such purchases help keep U.S. interest rates relatively low. For China, an undervalued valued currency has boosted exports and attracted foreign investment, but has lead to unbalanced economic growth and suppressed Chinese living standards.

The current global economic crisis has further complicated the currency issue for both the United States and China. Although China is under pressure from the United States to appreciate its currency, it is reluctant to do so because that could cause further damage to export sector and lead to more layoffs. China has halted its gradual appreciation of its currency, the renminbi (RMB) or yuan to the dollar in 2009, keeping it relatively constant at about 6.83 yuan per dollar. The federal budget deficit has increased rapidly since FY2008, causing a sharp increase in the amount of Treasury securities that must be sold. The Obama Administration has encouraged China to continue purchasing U.S. debt. However, if China were induced to further appreciate its currency against the dollar, it could slow its accumulation of foreign exchange reserves, thus reducing the need to invest in dollar assets, such as Treasury securities. Legislation has been introduced in the 111th Congress to address China's currency policy.

China's currency policy appears to have created a policy dilemma for the Chinese government. A strong and stable U.S. economy is in China's national interest since the United States is China's largest export market. Thus, some analysts contend that China will feel compelled to keep funding the growing U.S. debt. However, Chinese officials have expressed concern that the growing U.S. debt will eventually spark inflation in the United States and a depreciation of the dollar, which would negatively impact the value of China's holdings of U.S. securities. But if China stopped buying U.S. debt or tried to sell off a large portion of those holdings, it could also cause the dollar to depreciate and thus reduce the value of its remaining holdings, and such a move could further destabilize the U.S. economy. Chinese concerns over its large dollar holdings appear to have been reflected in a paper issued by the governor of the People's Bank of China, Zhou Xiaochuan on March 24, 2009, which called for replacing the U.S. dollar as the international reserve currency with a new global system controlled by the International Monetary Fund. China has also signed currency swap agreements with six of its trading partners, which would allow those partners to settle accounts with China using the yuan rather than the dollar.

Chapter 3 - Since the initiation of economic reforms 30 years ago, China has become one of the world's fastest-growing economies. From 1979 to 2008 China's real gross domestic product (GDP) grew at an average annual rate of nearly 10%; it grew 13% in 2007 (the fastest annual growth since 1994). However, the current global economic crisis has hit China hard – real GDP growth slowed to 9% in 2008, and many analysts predict the economy will slow even more sharply in 2009. Millions of workers have reportedly already lost their jobs. This is of great concern to the Chinese government, which views healthy economic growth as critical to maintaining social stability. China also faces a number of other challenges to its economic growth and stability, including pervasive government corruption, an inefficient banking system, over-dependence on exports and fixed investment for growth, the lack of rule of law, severe pollution, and widening income disparities. The Chinese government has indicated that it intends to create a "harmonious society" over the coming years that would promote more balanced economic growth and address a number of economic and social issues. The severity of the current global economic crisis has induced the Chinese government to seek means to quickly promote greater domestic demand; in November the government announced plans to implement a $586 billion economic stimulus package, largely aimed at infrastructure projects.

Trade and foreign investment plays a major role in China's booming economy. From 2004 to 2008, the value of total Chinese merchandise trade doubled. It is estimated that in 2008 China was the world's second largest merchandise exporter and the third largest importer. Over half of China's trade is conducted by foreign-invested firms in China. In 2008, foreign direct investment (FDI) in China totaled $92 billion, making it the third largest global destination for FDI. The combination of large trade surpluses, FDI flows, and large-scale purchases of foreign currency have helped make China the world's largest holder of foreign exchange reserves at $1.9 trillion at the end 2008. The global financial crisis is having a significant impact on China's trade, as exports and imports in November and December 2008 and January 2009 declined on a year-onyear basis. FDI flows have also declined sharply during this period.

China's economy and its economic policies are of major concern to many U.S. policymakers. On the one hand, U.S. consumers, exporters, and investors have greatly benefitted from China's rapid economic and trade growth. China's large holdings of U.S. securities have helped keep U.S. interest rates relatively low. Many analysts hope that China will make positive contributions to a global economic recovery. On the other hand, the surge in U.S. imports of Chinese products has put competitive pressures on various U.S. industries. Many U.S. policymakers have argued that China maintains a number of economic policies that violate its commitments in the World Trade Organization and/or are harmful to U.S. economic interests, such as its currency policy. Concerns have also been raised over China's rising demand for energy and raw materials (and the impact of that demand has on world prices), increased pollution levels, China's growing FDI (such as in energy and raw materials) around the world, including countries where the United States has political and human rights concerns, and the potential implications of China's large holdings of U.S. debt. The global economic crisis has also raised concerns over the future pace of Chinese economic reforms. This chapter provides an overview of China's economic development, challenges China faces to maintain growth, and the implications of China's rise as a major economic power for the United States.

The rapid rise of China as a major economic power within a time span of about 30 years is often described by analysts as one of the greatest economic success stories in modern times. From 1979 (when economic reforms began) to 2008, China's real gross domestic product (GDP) grew at an average annual rate of nearly 10%. From 1980 to 2008, China's economy grew14 fold in real terms, and real per capita GDP (a common measurement of living standards) grew over 11 fold. By some measurements, China is now the world's second largest economy and some analysts predict it could become the largest within a few decades.

China's economic rise has led to a substantial increase in U.S.-China economic ties. Total trade between the two countries surged from $5 billion in 1980 to $409 billion in 2008 (U.S. data). In 2008, China was the United States's second largest trading partner, its third largest export market, and its largest source of imports. Many U.S. companies have extensive operations in China in order to sell their products in the booming Chinese market and to take advantage of low-cost labor for export-oriented manufacturing. These operations have helped U.S. firms remain internationally competitive and have supplied U.S. consumers with a variety of low-cost goods. China's large-scale purchases of U.S. Treasury securities have enabled the federal government to fund its budget deficits, which helps keep U.S. interest rates relatively low.

However, the emergence of China as a major economic superpower has raised concern among many U.S. policymakers. Some express concern over the large and growing U.S. trade deficits with China, which rose from $10 billion in 1990 to $266 billion in 2008, and are viewed by many Members of Congress as an indicator that U.S.-Chinese commercial relations are imbalanced or unfair. Others claim that China uses unfair trade practices (such as an undervalued currency and subsidies to domestic producers) to flood U.S. markets with low-cost goods, and that such practices threaten American jobs, wages, and living standards.

China faces a number of significant economic challenges, including the fallout from the global financial crisis (which has slowed foreign demand for its exports and hence threatens economic growth), a weak banking system, widening income gaps, growing pollution, unbalanced economic growth (through over-reliance on exports and fixed investment), and widespread economic efficiencies resulting from non-market policies. The Chinese government views a growing economy as vital to maintaining social stability.

This chapter provides background on China's economic rise and current economic structure and the challenges China faces to keep its economy growing strong, and describes Chinese economic policies that are of concern to U.S. policymakers.

Chapter 4 - The People's Republic of China (PRC) is enjoying rapid economic growth. Real GDP grew at an annualized rate of 11.5 percent during the first half of 2007. Yet the PRC faces significant challenges that it must overcome to sustain longterm economic growth. These include:

- Unbalanced growth
- Corruption
- Weak financial services sector
- Severe environmental degradation
- Stress on the international economy

President Hu Jintao and other senior Chinese leaders have struggled to address these issues in preparation for the 17th National Congress of the Communist Party of China that convened in Beijing on October 15, 2007.

Chapter 5 - For a decade prior to 2005, the People's Republic of China (PRC) pegged its currency, the renminbi, to the U.S. dollar. On July 21 of that year, the PRC finally broke this peg. However, the PRC has continued to intervene heavily in foreign exchange markets to limit the subsequent appreciation of the renminbi. Governments in other Asian economies have sought to limit the appreciation of their currencies against both the renminbi and the U.S. dollar to maintain the price competitiveness of their manufactured exports with their Chinese rivals in North American and European markets. Shadowing the PRC's exchange rate policy, other Asian governments have also intervened heavily in foreign exchange markets. From 2001 to 2007, the PRC, India, Indonesia, Japan, South Korea, Malaysia, Taiwan, and Thailand have collectively added $2.7 trillion to their foreign exchange reserves. About 2/3 of these reserves have been invested in U.S. dollar-denominated assets, primarily U.S. Treasury and agency debt securities.

Since 2000, the PRC's exchange rate policy and the shadow policies of other Asian governments slowed the depreciation of the U.S. dollar and lowered interest rates, particularly at the long end of the yield curve. By distorting market price signals, these policies have exacerbated a number of economic problems not only in the United States but also around the world:

- These policies have contributed to the growth of unsustainable imbalances in the international accounts of both the PRC and the United States.
- The PRC's massive accumulation of foreign exchange reserves is stoking rapidly rising inflation in China.

- Low long-term interest rates contributed to the housing price bubble during the first half of this decade. As the bubble approached its peak, reckless lending became rampant.
- The bursting of this bubble revealed significant overinvestment and malinvestment in housing in the United States as well as significant speculative excesses in credit markets around the world.

The inevitable unwinding of these imbalances, the liquidation of overinvestment and malinvestment in housing, and the restoration of confidence in credit markets may slow real GDP growth in the United States for several years.

Chapter 6 - China's rapid economic growth since 1979 has transformed it into a major economic power. Over the past few years, many analysts have contended that China could soon overtake the United States to become the world's largest economy, based on estimates of China's economy on a "purchasing power parity" (PPP) basis, which attempts to factor in price differences across countries when estimating the size of a foreign economy in U.S. dollars. However, in December 2007, the World Bank issued a study that lowered its previous 2005 PPP estimate of the size of China's economy by 40%. If these new estimates are accurate, it will likely be many years before China's economy reaches U.S. levels. The new PPP data could also have an impact on U.S. and international perceptions over other aspects of China's economy, including its living standards, poverty levels, and government expenditures, such as on the military.

In: The Chinese Economy
Editors: Benjamin A. Tyler pp.1-40
ISBN: 978-1-60876-937-7

Chapter 1

FIVE CHALLENGES THAT CHINA MUST OVERCOME TO SUSTAIN ECONOMIC GROWTH

Jim Saxton

EXECUTIVE SUMMARY

Although the Chinese economy is booming, the People's Republic of China (PRC) faces five major challenges to sustain rapid economic growth in the future:

- unfavorable demographics;
- corruption and a weak rule of law;
- financially distressed state-owned enterprises and state-influenced enterprises;
- a dysfunctional financial system; and
- domestic and international imbalances.

The PRC's response to these challenges will, of course, determine the future performance of the Chinese economy. However, since the Chinese economy is so large and well integrated into the global economy, the performance of the Chinese economy will also affect the performance of the United States and other economies in the world.

So far, the PRC's approach to reform has been incremental. This incremental approach may be reaching the limits of its effectiveness. The challenges that the PRC now confronts are deeply interrelated. A more comprehensive approach to reform is needed.

I. INTRODUCTION

Since 1979, reform has transformed the People's Republic of China (PRC) from an impoverished autarkic socialist economy into a vibrant mixed economy that is open to international trade and investment. This study describes the genesis of economic reform under Paramount Leader Deng Xiaoping from 1979 to 1992 and reviews the subsequent performance of the Chinese economy.

Despite its success, the PRC confronts five serious challenges that it must overcome to sustain rapid economic growth in the future:

- unfavorable demographics;
- corruption and a weak rule of law;
- financially distressed state-owned enterprises (SOEs) and state-influenced enterprises (SIEs);
- a dysfunctional financial system; and
- domestic and international imbalances.

The PRC's response to these challenges will, of course, determine the future performance of the Chinese economy. However, since the Chinese economy is so large and well integrated into the global economy, the performance of the Chinese economy will also affect the performance of the United States and other economies throughout the world.

So far, the PRC's approach to reform has been incremental. This study concludes that this incremental approach may be reaching the limits of its effectiveness. The economic challenges that the PRC now faces are deeply interrelated. A more comprehensive approach to reform is needed.

II. Genesis of Economic Reform

Between 1979 and 1992, the Communist Party of China (CPC) lost its political legitimacy. The excesses of the Cultural Revolution repulsed the Chinese people and eroded their belief in communism as an ideology.[1] The contrast between the rapid development of the Japanese, South Korean, and other market-oriented economies in northeast and southeast Asia and the lack of development in the Chinese economy demonstrated the failure of communism as an economic system. Finally, the fall of the Berlin Wall in 1989 and the dissolution of the Soviet Union in 1991 undermined their confidence in communism as a political system.

Paramount Leader Deng Xiaoping was determined to preserve the communist regime in the PRC. After careful study, Deng identified several policy errors that contributed to the failure of the Soviet Union and its satellites:

- The Soviet economy could not sustain the costs of the Soviet Union's global military confrontation with the United States during the Cold War.
- The liberalization of the political system in Soviet Union and its satellites before economic reforms could produce prosperity allowed dissatisfied electorates to vote the communists out of power.

To regain political legitimacy, Deng decided that the CPC must transform its image, so that the Chinese people would perceive the CPC as the provider of their economic prosperity. Deng realized that an autarkic socialist economy could not deliver prosperity. Therefore, Deng concluded that the PRC had to adopt market-oriented economic policies and institutions and open itself to international trade and investment.

While immediate and sweeping policy changes would have sped the transformation of the PRC into a market economy, a "big bang" approach to reform would have also caused severe short-term dislocations during the transition. Unlike the former Soviet satellites, the CPC could have not blamed these transition costs on a previous regime. Moreover, any overt rejection of communism may have triggered a coup attempt among hardliners within the CPC.

Therefore, Deng decided to introduce economic policy changes gradually. Experiments were to be conducted in special economic zones, revised on the basis of results, and then adopted throughout the PRC. This incremental approach to reform would allow the CPC leadership sufficient time to isolate and neutralize opponents and to redefine communism. Indeed, the CPC has subsequently displayed remarkable ideological flexibility (e.g., describing market economics as socialism with Chinese characteristics).

During his trip to southern China during the spring of 1992, Deng proclaimed a "bargain" that still guides the PRC today:

- Domestically, the PRC would liberalize the economy to provide prosperity to the Chinese people, while the PRC would suppress political dissent.
- Internationally, the PRC would pursue "peaceful development" by:
  - opening itself to international trade and investment;
  - being a "good neighbor" in Asia;
  - avoiding direct military confrontations with the United States; and
  - securing access to oil and other natural resources even if the PRC must deal with rogue regimes.

The PRC rejected the failed import-substitution development strategies that India and Latin America had pursued in the 1970s and 1980s and instead copied the successful export- promotion development strategies of the Japanese, South Korean, and other economies in northeast and southeast Asia. The PRC relied on exports and foreign direct investment to:

- introduce the price system;
- correctly align domestic incentives; and
- import needed management skills and technology.

The PRC sought to exploit its comparative advantage in abundant low-cost labor with:

- labor-intensive manufacturing of low-tech goods (e.g., apparel, footwear, sporting goods, and toys) for export; and
- labor-intensive final assembly of medium-tech consumer electronics and information technology products from imported parts for export.

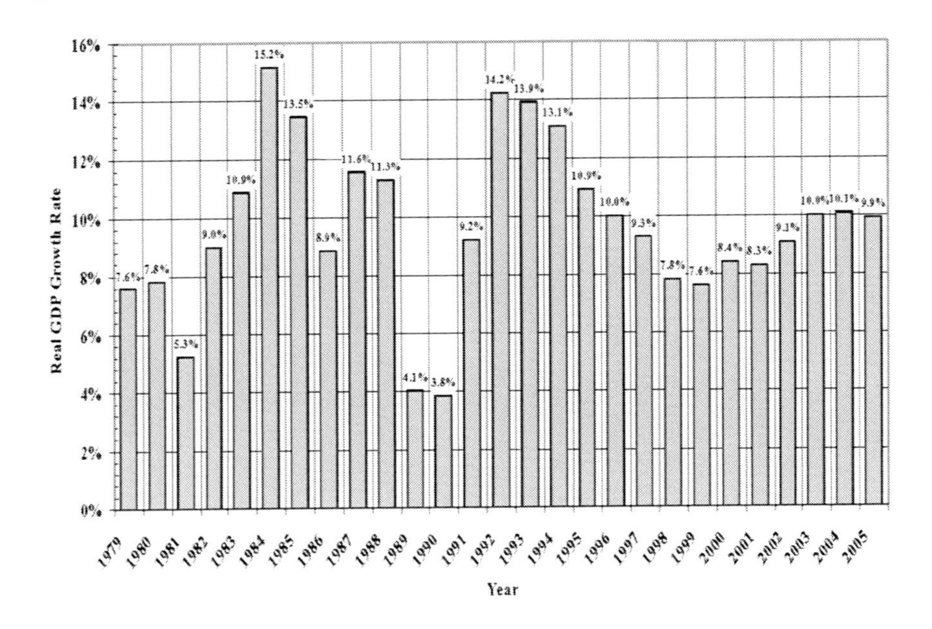

Graph 1. Real GDP Growth Rate in the People's Republic of China, 1979-2005

III. Results of Economic Reform

Reform has boosted the PRC's economy and improved the living standards of its people. Real GDP growth averaged 9.7 percent from 1979 to 2005 (see Graph 1).[2] In the first half of 2006, the Chinese economy grew at an annualized rate of 10.9 percent. This growth has lifted 400 million Chinese out of poverty.[3]

Reform has made the PRC a major trading power. In 1979, the PRC accounted for 1.3 percent of the world's two-way trade in goods (see Graph 2).[4] Real growth in the PRC's two-way trade in goods averaged 13.7 percent from 1979 to 2005.[5] By 2005, the PRC accounted for 8.8 percent of the world's two- way trade in goods (see Graph 2).[6]

While the PRC's trade performance may seem outstanding, it is actually quite typical for economies in northeast and southeast Asia that followed an export-promotion development strategy. During the twenty-six years after the takeoff of their economies, Japan, South Korea, and Singapore had similar or better trade performances than the PRC (see Graph 3).[7]

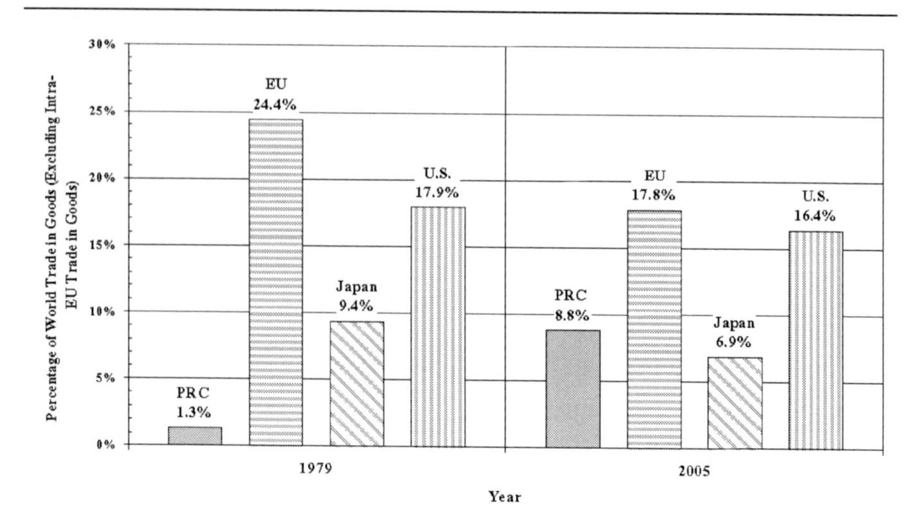

Graph 2. Rise of the People's Republic of China as a Trading Power, 1979 to 2005

The PRC's heavy reliance on foreign direct investment (FDI) distinguishes its development strategy and its post-takeoff performance From other populous economies in northeast and southeast Asia.[8] From 1979 to 2005, the PRC received a cumulative $633 billion of FDI on a historical cost basis (see Graph 4).[9]

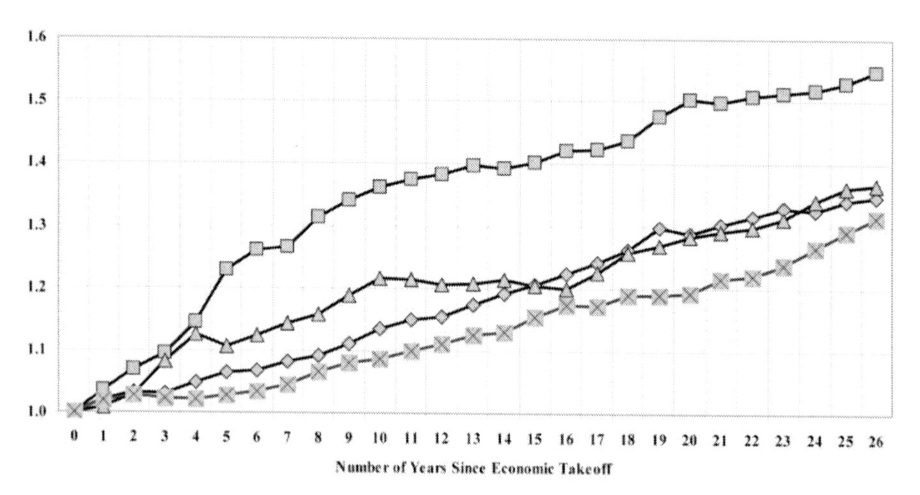

Graph 3. Growth of Real Goods Exports from Japan, South Korea, Singapore, and the People's Republic of China in the 26 Years since Economic Takeoffs (Index, Year of Economic Takeoff = 0, Log Scale)

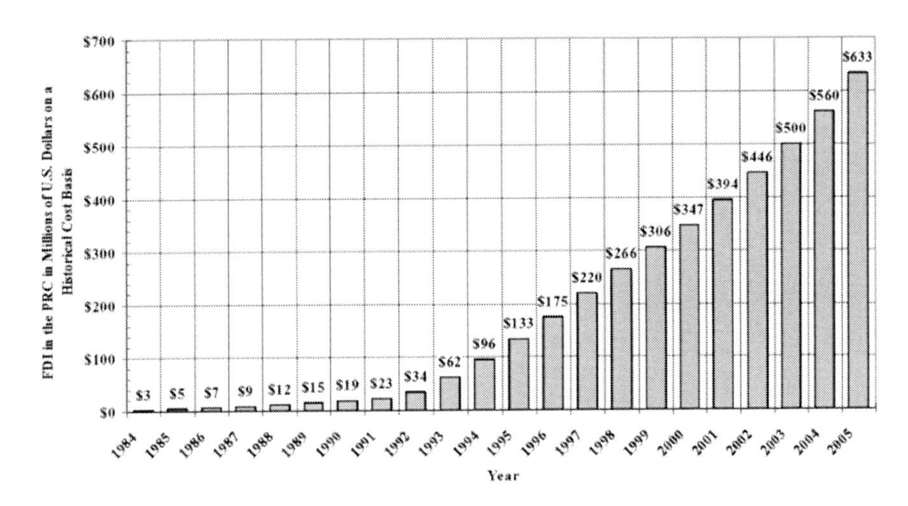

Graph 4. Cumulative Foreign Direct Investment (FDI) in the People's Republic of China, 1982-2005

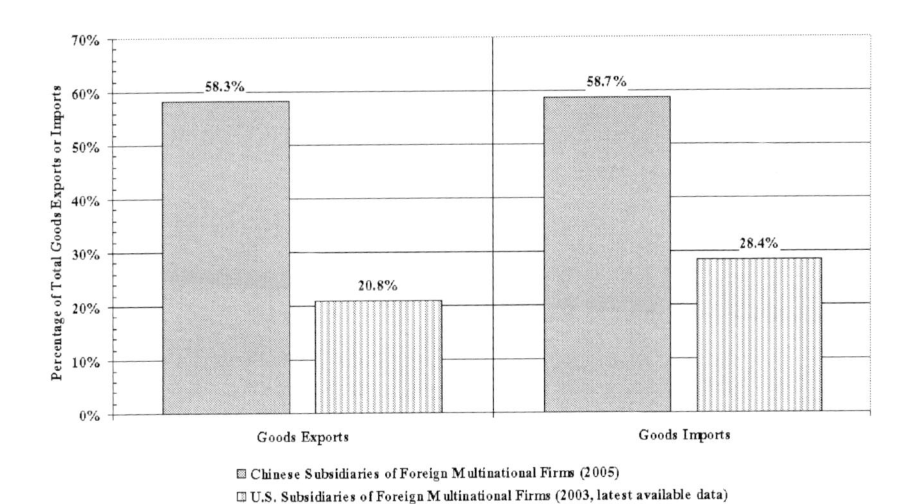

Graph 5. The PRC's Goods Trade is Heavily Dependent on Chinese Subsidiaries of Foreign Multinational Firms

The Chinese subsidiaries of foreign multinational firms produced 19.1 percent of the PRC's value-added for industrial firms in 2003 (the last year in which comprehensive firm-level data are available)[10] and accounted for 58.3 percent of the PRC's exports of goods and 58.7 percent of its imports of goods in 2005 (see Graph 5).[11] Unlike Japan or South Korea twenty-six years after the takeoff of their economies, the PRC has spawned relatively few Chinese multinational firms that manufacture own-design, own-brand goods for global markets.

IV. UNFAVORABLE DEMOGRAPHICS

The first challenge that the PRC must overcome is unfavorable demographics. Without significant immigration, the PRC's declining fertility rate will cause its working-age population to peak in 2015 and then decline. Simultaneously, the PRC's increasing longevity rate will swell both the number of the elderly and the elderly as a percentage of total population.

A. Declining Labor Force

Because of the PRC's one-child policy and rising per capita income, the PRC's fertility rate fell to 1.70 per woman during 2000-2005 -- well below the population maintenance rate (see Graph 6). Consequently, the PRC's working-age population (ages 15-64) will peak in 2015 and then begin to shrink (see Graph 7).[12]

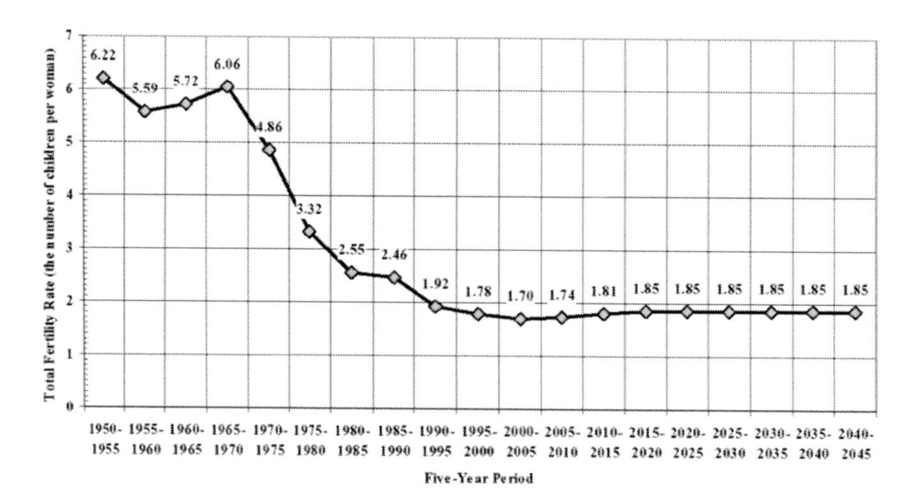

Graph 6. The PRC's One-Child Policy Pushes the PRC's Fertility Rate Below Population Maintenance Rate, 1950-1955 to 2040-2045

In major cities, the economic boom has already created a shortage of highly skilled workers and professionals, boosting their real compensation. The *Financial Times* recently reported:

> *"Five years ago, to employ an engineer in China cost a tenth of the figure in the U.S.," says Michael Marks, chairman of Flextronics, a U.S.-listed company that is the world's second biggest contract manufacturer for the electronics industry. "Today the difference is only half."*[13]

Real compensation for less skilled or unskilled workers has also begun to grow, but at a slower pace. Because of higher labor costs, the "China price" – the price that major retailers (e.g., Walmart, Carefour) are willing to pay to their suppliers based on the cost of importing similar goods from China – increased for the first time in 2005.[14]

Currently, the PRC has a "floating population" of about 140 million unemployed or underemployed people. At the PRC's current growth rate, however, these "floaters" will be fully absorbed into the economy by 2015.

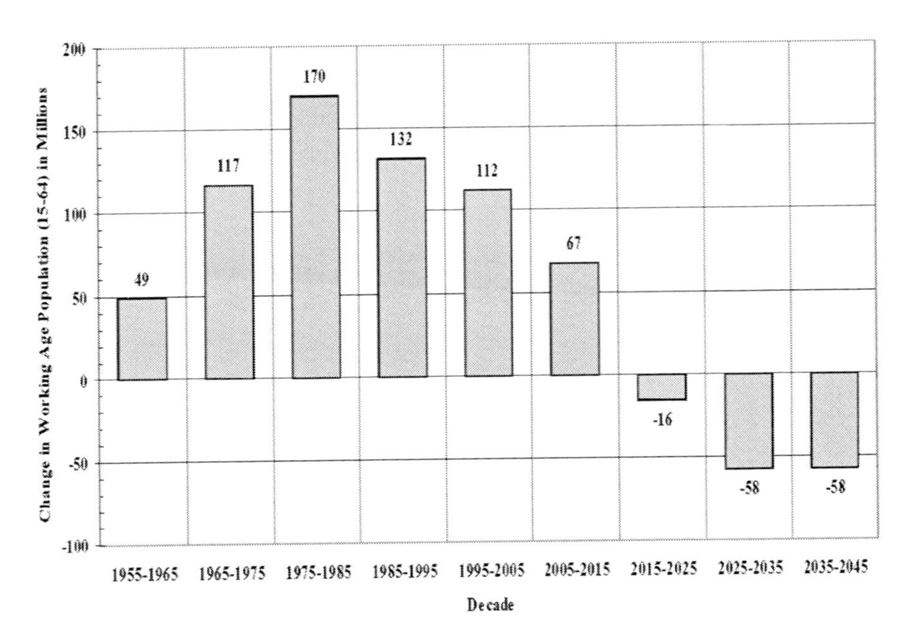

Graph 7. The PRC's Working Age Population (15-64) Will Soon Peak and Then Decline, 1955-1965 to 2035-2045

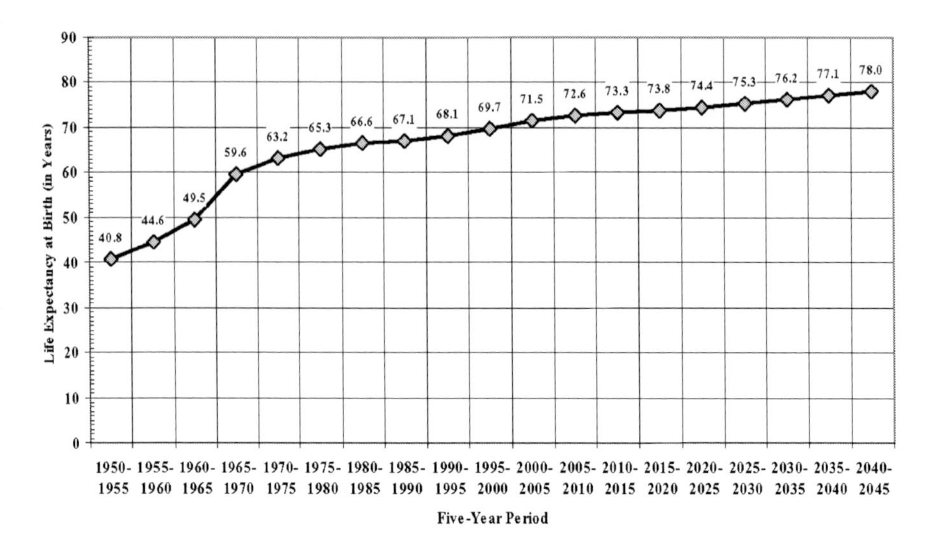

Graph 8. Increase of Longevity in the People's Republic of China, 1950-1955 to 2040-2045

Consequently, the PRC cannot remain a low-wage economy. After 2015, labor shortages should significantly increase the real compensation of all Chinese workers. This will force the PRC to shed many of its current jobs in labor-intensive industries and assembly operations. To foster continued economic growth, the PRC will need to climb the “development ladder” by

- encouraging Chinese firms to develop their own brands and designs;
- switching from labor-intensive to capital-intensive manufacturing; and
- expanding the service sector.

B. Graying Population

Higher living standards have boosted the PRC’s life expectancy at birth to 71.5 years during 2000-05 (see Graph 8).[15] Since the increase in longevity is expected to continue, the PRC’s elderly population should increase from 100 million, or 7.6 percent of the total population, to 320 million, or 23.0 percent of the total population, in 2045.[16] Consequently, the elderly support ratio (i.e., the ratio of elderly Chinese to working-age Chinese) is expected to drop from 9.3 in 2005 to 2.7 in 2045 (see Graph 9).[17]

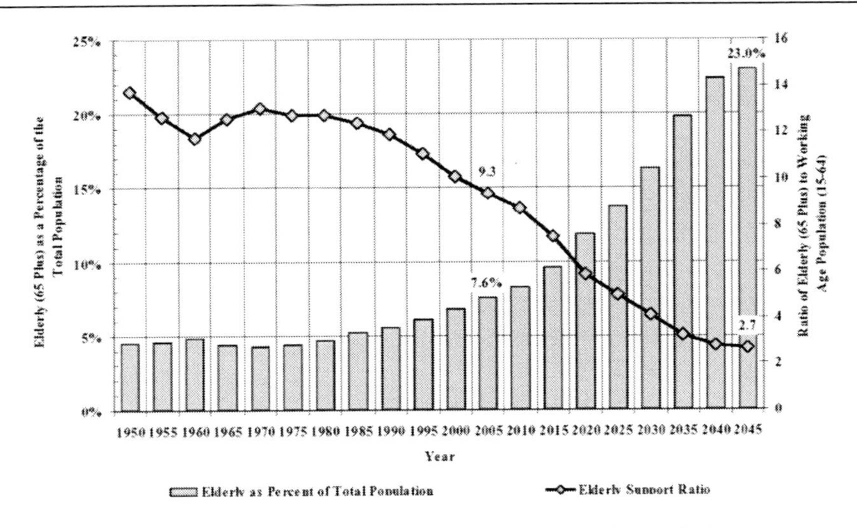

Graph 9. Lower Fertility and Higher Longevity is Increasing the PRC's Elderly Burden, 1950-2045

Unlike other major economies, the PRC lacks a comprehensive system of either government old-age pensions or private retirement saving plans. Reform eliminated Mao's "iron rice bowl" system under which state-owned enterprises provided their workers with comprehensive social-welfare benefits. Today, only 15 percent of urban workers are eligible for government old-age pensions.[18] Few private retirement plans are available. Consequently, the elderly must rely on their own savings or their family for retirement income.

Graph 10 - Gross Saving Rate in the People's Republic of China, 1982-2005

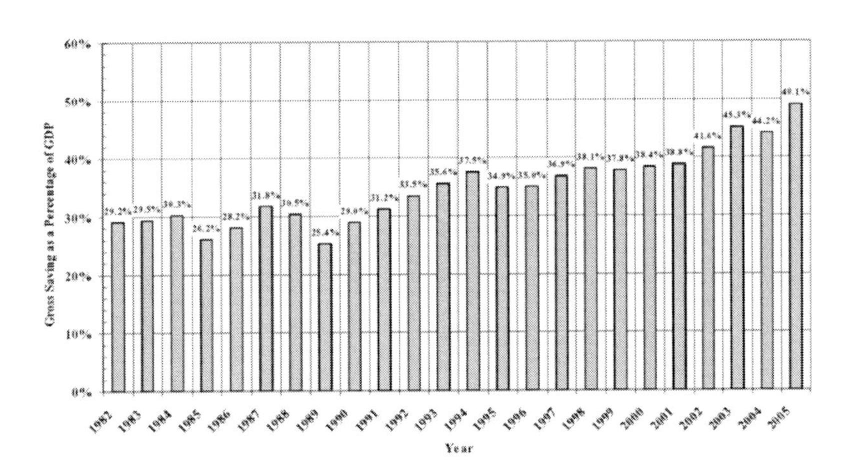

Graph 10. Gross Saving Rate in the People's Republic of China, 1982-2005

The lack of a government social safety net and the limited availability of consumer credit, insurance products, and private retirement plans drive Chinese households to save prodigious sums. In 2005, the PRC's gross saving rate was 49.1 percent of GDP (see Graph 10).[19] The PRC's gross saving rate is extraordinarily high compared to other major economies (see Graph 11). Until the PRC develops a comprehensive social safety net and deepens its market for financial services, Chinese households are unlikely to reduce their extraordinarily high saving rate. Consequently, the PRC may incur difficulties shifting from export-led to domestic consumption-driven economic growth.

V. CORRUPTION AND A WEAK RULE OF LAW

The PRC has adopted a "rule by law," but still lacks a "rule of law." Although there have been significant procedural improvements in the drafting of legislation,[20] many Chinese laws and regulations still lack clarity, their enforcement may be arbitrary, and courts are subject to political influence. Consequently, property rights are insecure.

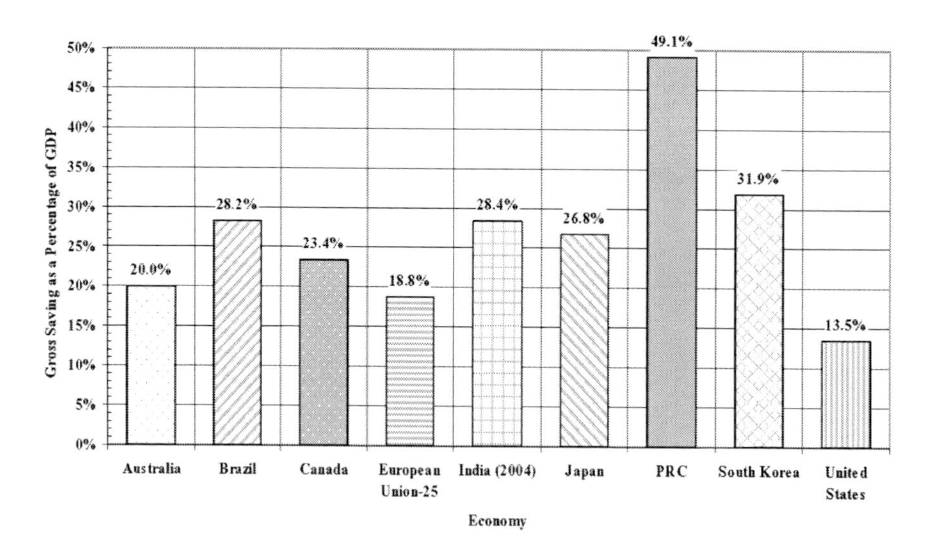

Graph 11. The PRC's Gross Saving Rate is Unusually High Compared to Other Major Economies, 2005

Individuals and private firms must rely on *guanxi* (i.e., connections) with officials to protect themselves and their property. During the last quarter century, economic reform has produced a *de facto* political decentralization that has allowed officials to exploit their *guanxi* to enrich themselves and their families through corruption.

While the PRC is nominally a unitary state, it has many levels of subsidiary government – provinces, prefectures, cities, counties, towns, and villages. The central government is quite small, employing about 500,000 of the estimated 36 million working in governmental functions.[21]

The PRC's government is organized as a matrix. Each department in the central government is paired with similar departments in subsidiary governments. Policy is vertical (i.e., the heads of central government departments in Beijing determine policy and direct its implementation through similar departments in subsidiary governments), but administration is horizontal (i.e., the heads of subsidiary governments make personnel decisions and fund the operations of all departments in their subsidiaries).

Under Mao, the PRC's government functioned as a hierarchal structure since the central government tightly controlled the economy. Reform has allowed local party leaders to acquire great wealth through legitimate business investments and various corrupt payments. Both legitimate tax receipts from a booming economy and corrupt payments have also reduced the financial dependency of subsidiary governments on central government transfers. Together these changes have limited the central government's ability to implement policy changes and control corrupt practices. Employees in local departments may have greater loyalty to local government officials and party leaders than to department heads in Beijing. The Chinese use an old proverb to describe this problem, "The mountain is high, and the emperor is far away."

Corruption is both widespread and costly in the PRC. Transparency International reported that the PRC scored 3.2 on its *Corruption Perceptions Index 2005* (10 is corruptionfree).[22] Chinese economist Angang Hu[23] estimated that corruption costs the PRC's government an amount to equal 15 percent of GDP in lost revenue and skimmed funds.[24] The *China Economic Quarterly* (2005) reported that provincial and local government officials extracted the equivalent of 91 percent of the profits of private firms in 2003 through non-tax costs, including fees, *tanpai* (i.e., forced expenditures on unwanted provincial or local goods or services), or *zhaodai* (i.e., the entertainment of provincial or local government officials).[25]

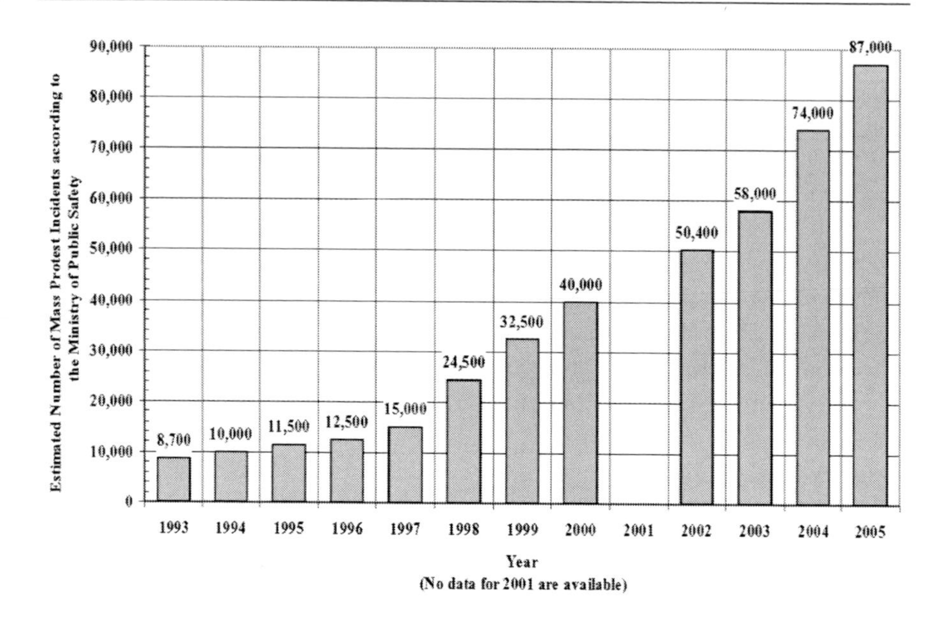

Graph 12. Mass Protest Incidents in the PRC, 1993-2005

Indigenous creative industries could create new high-skill, high-wage jobs to replace the low-skill, low-wage jobs in labor-intensive manufacturing and assembly operations that the PRC is likely to lose in future years. However, corruption stifles the development of indigenous creative industries that depend on secure intellectual property rights.

Corruption, particularly the uncompensated seizure of land for development, fuels growing unrest. The reported number of mass protests soared ten-fold over twelve years, reaching 87,000 protests in 2005 (see Graph 12).[26] The central government has responded to the growing number of mass protests by:

- acknowledging problems;
- appeasing ordinary protestors by making superficial changes (e.g., dismissing and prosecuting corrupt local officials); and
- punishing protest leaders to prevent local protests from coalescing into a national movement.

So far, the central government has been able to contain local protests. How successful this strategy will be in future is difficult to predict.

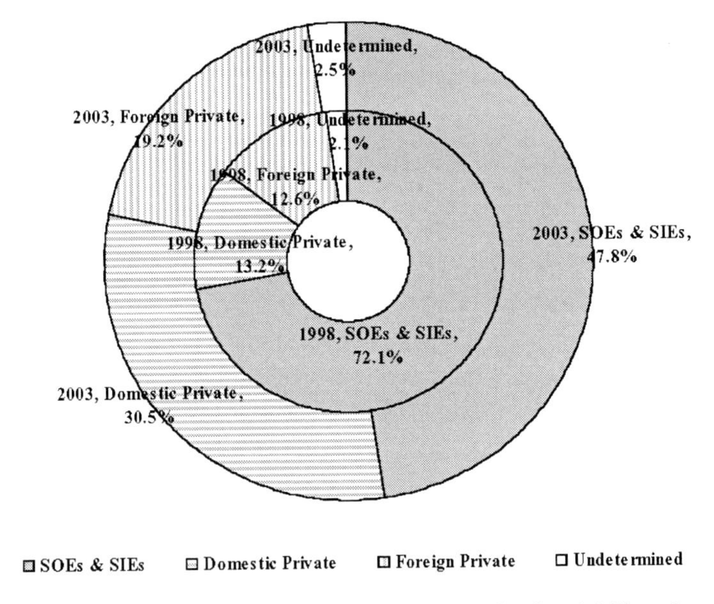

Graph 13. Growing Private Sector Output: Value-Added of Industrial Firms by Enterprise Type in the PRC, 1998 and 2003

VI. Financially Distressed State-Owned Enterprises and State- Influenced Enterprises

Early economic reforms that introduced the price system and profit incentives to the SOEs did not significantly improve their performance. Consequently, President Jiang Zemin announced the *zhuada fangxiao* policy (i.e., grab the big, dump the small) at the Fifteenth Party Congress in 1997. Under this policy, the central government retained ownership of state-owned enterprises that:

- produce defense goods and services;
- are in industrial sectors targeted for economic development; or
- are hopelessly insolvent, but employ millions.

The central government has transformed many of the large state-owned enterprises that it had retained into shareholding enterprises by issuing minority shares to investors. While shareholding enterprises exhibit many of the characteristics of private corporations, the central government still exercises effective control over their operations. At year-end 2005, the central government still controlled 66 percent of the market value of all shareholding enterprises through non-marketable shares. In the *Australian Financial Review*, Stephen Wyatt concluded:

> *In fact, the entire privatization of China's state-owned enterprises is still more hype than reality. ... The government's strategy is still to list minority shares in state-owned groups in order to raise capital and import better governance while ultimately retaining control ...*[27]

The remaining small- and medium-sized state-owned enterprises were converted into a variety of state-influenced enterprises:

- Township and village enterprises (TVEs) in rural areas;
- Cooperative enterprises owned by their employees;
- Collective enterprises owned by provincial governments and local governments in urban areas;
- Private domestic enterprises often sold to officials or their families; and
- Joint enterprises owned by a state-owned enterprise in conjunction with another type of enterprises.

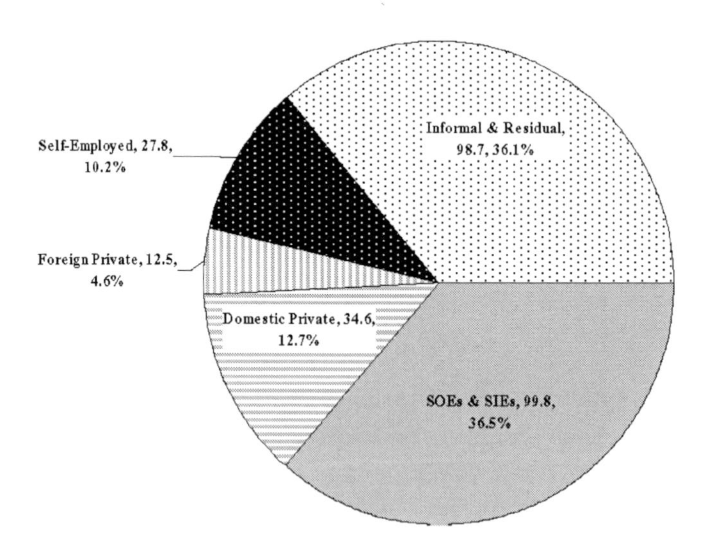

Graph 14. Employment in Urban China, 2005 (in millions and as a percentage of total urban employment)

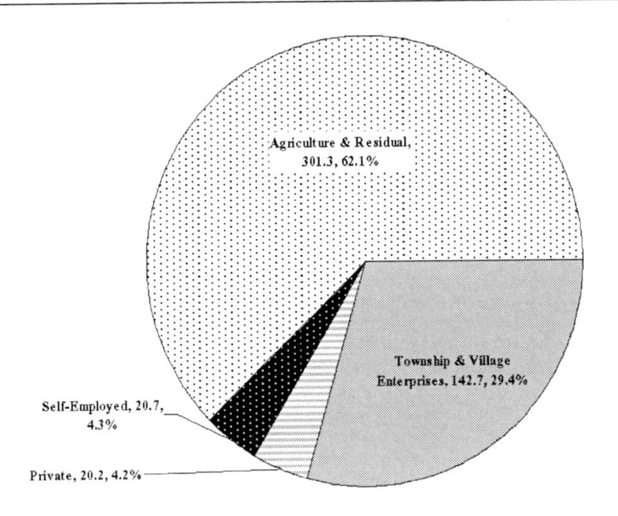

Graph 15. Employment in Rural China, 2005 (in millions and as a percentage of total rural employment)

SOEs and SIEs remain a major part of the PRC's economy:

- Producing 47.8 percent of the value-added among industrial firms in the PRC during 2003 (see Graph 13);[28]
- Employing 99.8 million in urban areas during 2005 (see Graph 14);[29]
- Employing 142.7 million in rural areas during 2005 (see Graph 15);[30] and
- Accounting for 74.1 percent of the PRC's investment in fixed assets during 2005 (see Graph 16).[31] SOEs and SIEs are a significant source of patronage for the CPC. In 2003, SOEs and SIEs employed 5.3 million party members as executives or senior managers.[32]

However, SOEs and SIEs are notoriously inefficient. The Organization for Economic Cooperation and Development (OECD) measured the total factor productivity (TFP) in a broad cross- section of firms in the PRC. TFP refers to the portion of the increase in economic output that cannot be attributed to increases in the quantity or the quality of factor inputs. Thus, TFP represents the gains in output from efficiency and innovation. The OECD found that the TFP of private Chinese firms and Chinese subsidiaries of foreign multinational firms is double the TFP of SOEs and one and one-half times the TFP of SIEs during 1998-2003 after controlling for size, location, and industry (see Graph 17).[33]

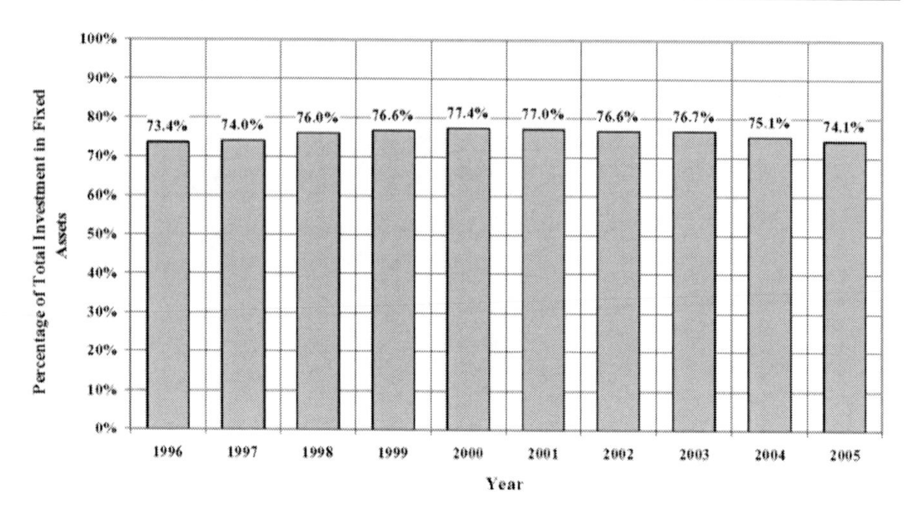

Graph 16. SOE & SIE Investment in Fixed Assets as a Percentage of Total Investment in Fixed Assets, 1996-2005

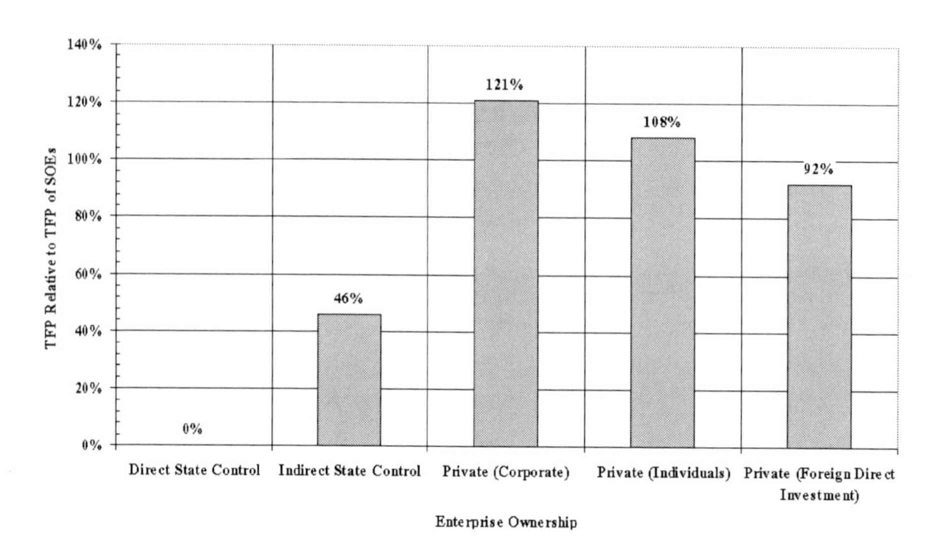

Graph 17. Relative Level of Total Factor Productivity of Various Enterprise Types to Total Factor Productivity of State-Owned Enterprises, 1998-2003

Consequently, the average return on equity was 6.7 percent in all SOEs during 2003.[34] Moreover, the OECD found insolvent or unprofitable SOEs and SIEs accounted for 11 percent of the workers, 23 percent of the fixed assets, and 22 percent of the outstanding debt in all SOEs and SIEs. Marginally profitable SOEs and SIEs accounted for 9 percent of the workers, 7 percent of the fixed assets, and 18 percent of the outstanding debt in all SOEs and SIEs. When combined, these financially distressed SOEs and SIEs accounted for 20 percent of the workers, 30 percent of the fixed assets, and 40 percent of the outstanding debt in all SOEs and SIEs (see Graph 18).[35]

SOEs and SIEs use their *guanxi* to secure favorable regulations and preferential access to loans from Chinese banks and other depository institutions. Consequently, many SOEs and SIEs face a "soft budget constraint" (i.e. Chinese banks and other depository institutions lend to the SOEs and SIEs without regard to their ability to repay their loans). Non-market loans allow many financially distressed SOEs and SIEs to continue operations and invest in new fixed assets when market discipline would force these SOEs and SIEs to shutter operations or to forego the acquisition of fixed assets.

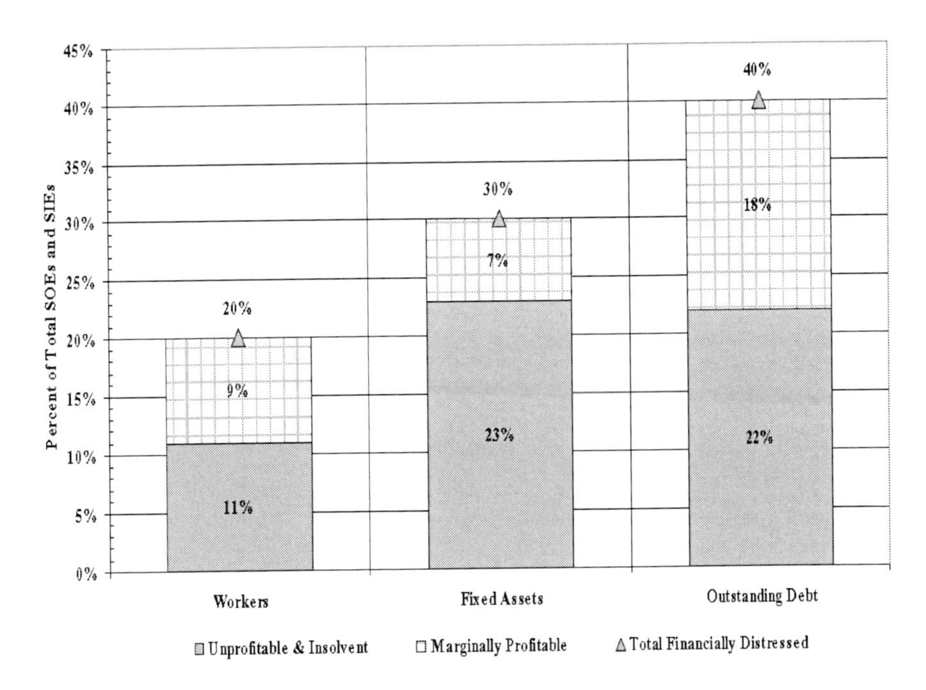

Graph 18. Workers, Fixed Assets, and Outstanding Debt in Financially Distressed SOEs and SIEs in the PRC

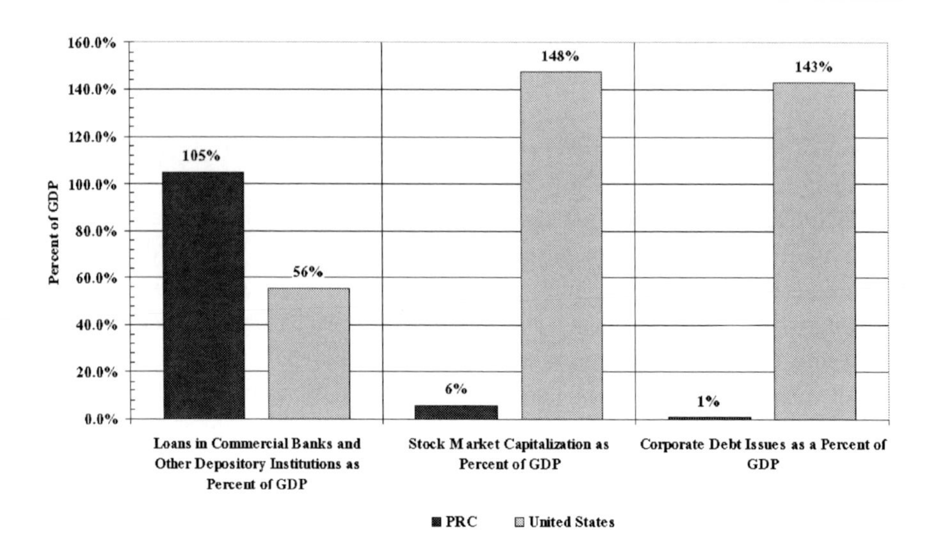

Graph 19. The PRC's Financial System is Bank-Centric (Year-End 2005, Corporate Debt Securities Year-End 2004)

VII. A DYSFUNCTIONAL FINANCIAL SYSTEM

A. Bank-Centric, State-Directed Financial System

The PRC's financial system is very bank-centric. At year-end 2004, corporate debt issues amounted to 1 percent of GDP in China compared to 143 percent of GDP in the United States.[36] At year-end 2005, equity issues (marketable shares) amounted to 6 percent of GDP in China compared to 148 percent of GDP in the United States;[37] and loans at banks and other depository institutions amounted to 105 percent of GDP in China compared to 56 percent of GDP in the United States (see Graph 19).[38]

Banking assets are highly concentrated in the PRC (see Graph 20). The four major state- owned commercial banks – the Agricultural Bank of China, the Bank of China, China Construction Bank, and the Industrial Commercial Bank of China – controlled 57.1 percent of banking assets at year-end 2005.[39] Twelve joint stock commercial banks[40] controlled another 16.8 percent of banking assets at year-end 2005.[41]

Despite some progress in developing credit evaluation and risk management skills, non- market criteria may still influence over one-half of lending decisions. This occurs through both *guanxi* loans[42] and policy loans.[43] Non-market lending affects the overall composition of the loan portfolios in Chinese banks and other depository institutions. While banks in other economies extend most of their loans to households and small- to medium-sized private firms, 64.5 percent of outstanding loans in the PRC at year-end 2005 were extended to SOEs and SIEs (see Graph 21).[44]

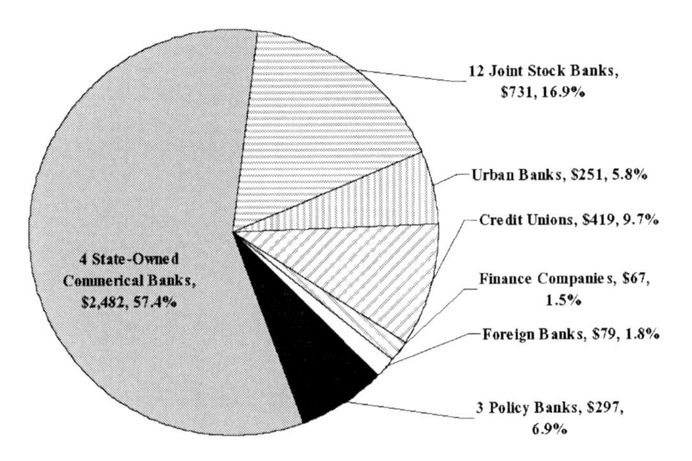

Graph 20. Banking is Concentrated in the PRC Assets in Types of Banks and Other Depository Institutions in Billions of U.S. Dollars and as a Percentage of Assets in All Banks and Other Depository Institutions as of Year-End 2005

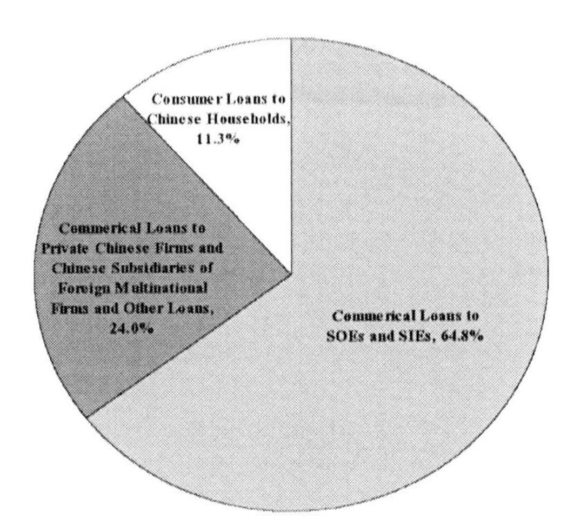

Graph 21. Outstanding Loans by Type as a Percentage of Total Outstanding Loans at Banks and Other Depository Institutions in the PRC, Year-End 2005

Centrally directed industrial policy still governs the issuance of debt and equity securities in the PRC. The State Council -- the equivalent of the President's cabinet in the United States -- must approve the issuance of all equity securities on Chinese stock exchanges. The National Development and Reform Commission, which is the PRC's industry policy agency and reports to the State Council, must approve the issuance of all corporate debt securities. Consequently, nearly all of the proceeds from corporate debt and equity issues in the PRC have gone to SOEs and SIEs.[45]

B. Economic Costs of Non-Market Allocation of Financing

In a recent study of the PRC's financial system, Farrell et al. (2006) found that the non- market allocation of financing harms the Chinese economy in two ways:

- Non-market allocation of financing reduced the potential size of the PRC's GDP by $321 billion a year or about 14 percent of its current GDP;[46] and
- Non-market allocation of financing has slashed the average real return on savings in the PRC to a mere 0.5 percent over the last decade. This compares to an average real return on savings in the United States of 3.1 percent over the same period.[47]

C. Nonperforming Loans

Chinese banks and other depository institutions had a large legacy of nonperforming loans from non-market lending to SOEs and SIEs prior to 1999. Approximately $170 billion of nonperforming loans have been transferred from the four major state-owned commercial banks to four asset management companies during 1999 and 2000.[48] So far, the asset management companies have disposed of 67 percent of these nonperforming loans, recovering about 21¢ on $1 of face value. Another $136 billion of nonperforming loans have been transferred to asset management companies during the last two years.

Both Chinese officials and private economists acknowledge that the PRC has done a good job in identifying and resolving pre-1999 nonperforming loans in Chinese banks and other depository institutions. However, Chinese officials and private economists disagree about the current size of the nonperforming loan problem in the PRC. In particular, Chinese officials and private economists have differences of opinion on how many loans made by Chinese banks and other depository institutions since 1998 are now or will become nonperforming loans.

The China Banking Regulatory Commission reported that nonperforming loans in commercial banks have fallen to $164 billion, or 6.6 percent of GDP as of March 31, 2006.[49] Nonperforming loans in other depository institutions amounted to $42 billion, or 1.7 percent of GDP as of March 31, 2006.[50]

In a widely publicized study, Ernst & Young estimated that nonperforming loans amounted to $911 billion, or 41 percent of GDP at year-end 2005.[51] The People's Bank of China and the China Banking Regulatory Commission vigorously disputed the Ernst & Young estimate. Under pressure from Chinese officials, Ernst & Young, which audits the Bank of China and the Industrial Commercial Bank of China, withdrew its study nine days after its release.[52]

However, the withdrawn Ernst & Young estimate is broadly in line with other private estimates. As of March 31, 2006, for example, Fitch Ratings estimated that commercial banks and other depository institutions had another $270 billion of problem loans in addition to $164 billion of officially reported nonperforming loans in commercial banks, $42 billion of officially reported nonperforming loans in other depository institutions, and $197 billion of nonperforming loans remaining in the asset management companies.[53] If all of the estimated problem loans become nonperforming, then nonperforming loans would equal $673 billion, or 27.3 percent of GDP as of March 31, 2006.

Because of insecure property rights, capricious zoning, arbitrary inspections, and widespread corruption, individuals and private firms without strong *guanxi* with the government and party officials cannot easily participate in the real estate industry. Thus, most construction firms and developers in the PRC are SOEs or SIEs. Real estate speculation is now rampant in major Chinese cities. On June 13, 2006, *Business Week* recently reported:

> *People's Bank of China deputy governor Wu Xiaoling has warned publicly that the value of total private and commercial investment in real estate shot up from about 2.5 percent of total gross domestic product in 2001 to 8.6 percent in 2005. "Real estate bubbles will affect the economy and people's lives seriously, especially when bubbles burst,"*[54]

In the last few years, Chinese banks and other depository institutions have aggressively lent to SOEs and SIEs for construction and real estate development. This explosive loan growth may be creating mountains of new nonperforming loans in Chinese banks and other depository institutions that bank and government officials have not yet recognized.

D. Recapitalization

To recapitalize ailing banks, the PRC's central bank, the People's Bank of China, injected $60 billion of foreign exchange reserves into the four major state-owned commercial banks between 2003 and 2005. During 2005, foreign financial services firms invested $18 billion in minority shares in Chinese banks (see Table 1).

An initial public offering (IPO) of 13 percent of the shares raised $9.2 billion for the China Construction Bank in October 2005, while an IPO of 10.5 percent of the shares raised $9.7 billion for the Bank of China in May 2006. During the rest of 2006, IPOs are expected to raise about $10 billion for the Industrial Commercial Bank of China, $2 billion for the China Merchants Bank, $1 billion for the Minsheng Bank, and $1 billion for the CITIC Bank.

In March 2006, the *Economist Intelligence Unit* observed:

> *[Q]uestions remain over whether risk management standards in the banking sector have improved in a way that would prevent such problems from re-emerging. One particular problem is the government's strong control over lending patterns, which encourages capital to be allocated on the basis of policy rather than profit.*[55]

Senior PRC officials face a conundrum. If the government were to cede its control over Chinese banks, they would curtail their non-market lending and strengthen their balance sheets. Market lending would use Chinese saving more efficiently. Consequently, the PRC's long-term real GDP growth would be higher, and Chinese households would earn a better return on their savings. However, curtailing non-market lending would cause many financially distressed SOEs and SIEs to fail, leading to higher unemployment in the short run. These short-term dislocations could break the "bargain" that has kept the CPC in power.

Table 1. Foreign Direct Investment in Chinese Banks

Chinese Banks	Foreign Investors	Ownership
Industrial Commercial Bank of China	Goldman Sachs, American Express, & Allianz Group	10%
China Construction Bank	Bank of America	8.67% (may increase to 19.9%)
	Temasek Holdings	5.98%
Bank of China	Royal Bank of Scotland	10%
	Merrill Lynch, Li Ka-Shing, & Temasek Holdings	10%
	UBS	1.6%
	Asian Development Bank	0.24%
Bank of Communications	HSBC	19.9%
Shanghai Pudong Development Bank	Citigroup	4.6% (may increase to 24.9%)
Minsheng Bank	IFC	0.93%
	Temasek Holdings	3.9%
Industrial Bank	Hang Seng Bank	15.98%
	IFC	4%
	Singapore Investment	5%
Hu Xia Bank	Deutsche Bank	9.9%
	Sal Oppenheim	4.08%
	Pangaea Capital Management	6.9%
Shenzhen Development Bank	Newbridge Capital	17.98% (will drop)
	GE Capital	7.3% (pending)
Guangdong Development Bank	Citigroup	Seeking 85%
Beijing Bank	ING Group	19.9%
	IFC	5%
Shanghai Bank	HSBC	8%
	IFC	7%
Nanjing City Commercial Bank	IFC	5%
	BNP	19.2%
Tiajin Bohai Bank	Standard Chartered	19.99%
Hangzhou City Commercial Bank	Commonwealth Bank of Australia	19.99%
Jinan City Commercial Bank	Commonwealth Bank of Australia	11%
Xian City Commercial Bank	IFC	2.5%
	Bank of Nova Scotia	2.5%
Ping An Bank	HSBC	27%
Nanchong City Commercial Bank	DEG	10%
	SIDT	3.3%
Ningbo City Commercial Bank	Oversea-Chinese Banking Corp.	12.2%

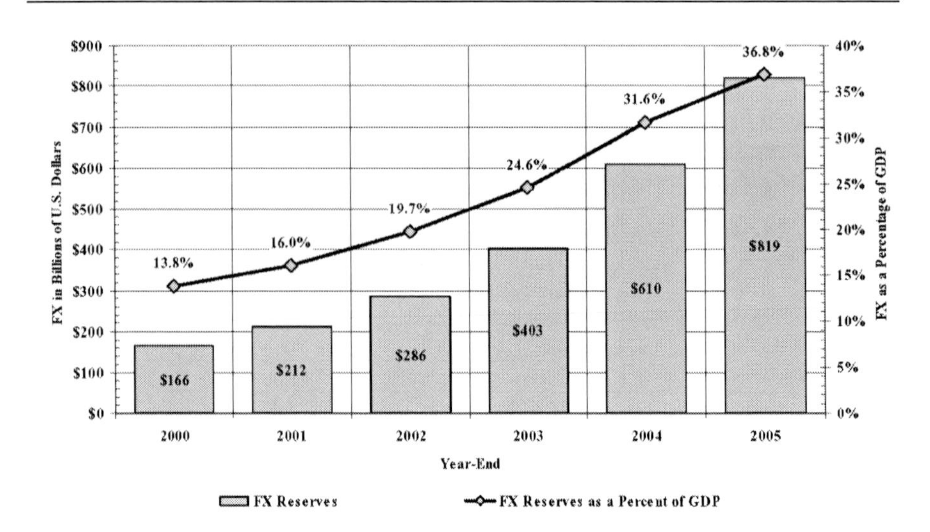

Graph 22. The People's Bank of China's Foreign Exchange Reserves in Billions of U.S. Dollars and as a Percentage of GDP, Year-End 2000-2005

Non-market lending may buy political stability for a time. However, in its accession agreement with the World Trade Organization, the PRC committed to open its domestic banking market to foreign banks in 2007, allowing them make loans to and receive deposits from all Chinese households and firms in yuan. Implementing this commitment will create a viable alternative to Chinese banks and other depository institutions for Chinese households and firms.

Unlike the United States, the central government does not insure deposits in Chinese banks and other depository institutions. If financial weaknesses are allowed to fester, runs, in which a large number of depositors suddenly attempt to withdraw all of their funds from Chinese banks and place them in "safer" foreign banks, could soon occur. Runs could cause some Chinese banks to fail. To avert a financial panic and a possible recession, the People's Bank of China and the central government would likely be forced to bail out failing banks.

VIII. Domestic and International Imbalances

On July 21, 2005, the PRC broke its previous peg with the U.S. dollar, revalued the renminbi[56] by 2.1 percent, and instituted an adjustable exchange rate tied to a basket of currencies including the U.S. dollar. Prior to this change, the People's Bank of China actively intervened in foreign exchange markets to maintain the peg of the renminbi to U.S. dollar. Nevertheless, the People's Bank of China continued to actively intervene to limit any appreciation of the renminbi against the U.S. dollar. One year after this change, the renminbi has appreciated by only 3.56 percent against the U.S. dollar (from 1 yuan equal to 12.0824 U.S. cents on July 21, 2005, to 1 yuan equal to 12.5128 U.S. cents on July 20, 2006).[57]

Graph 22 shows the accumulation of foreign exchange reserves in terms of both U.S. dollars and as a percentage of the PRC's GDP. By year-end 2005, the People's Bank of China accumulated $819 billion, or 36.8 percent of GDP, in foreign exchange reserves. Through June 2006, the People's Bank of China accumulated foreign exchange reserves of $941 billion, an increase of 14.9 percent in just six months.[58]

Interventions of the People's Bank of China suppress the foreign exchange value of the renminbi below a market-determined level. In November 2005, Morris Goldstein at the Institute for International Economics estimated that the renminbi was undervalued by between 20 percent and 40 percent using an underlying balance approach and by between 20 percent and 30 percent using a global payments balance approach. This is broadly in line with the majority of private sector estimates.[59] This exchange rate policy contributes to both domestic and international balances.

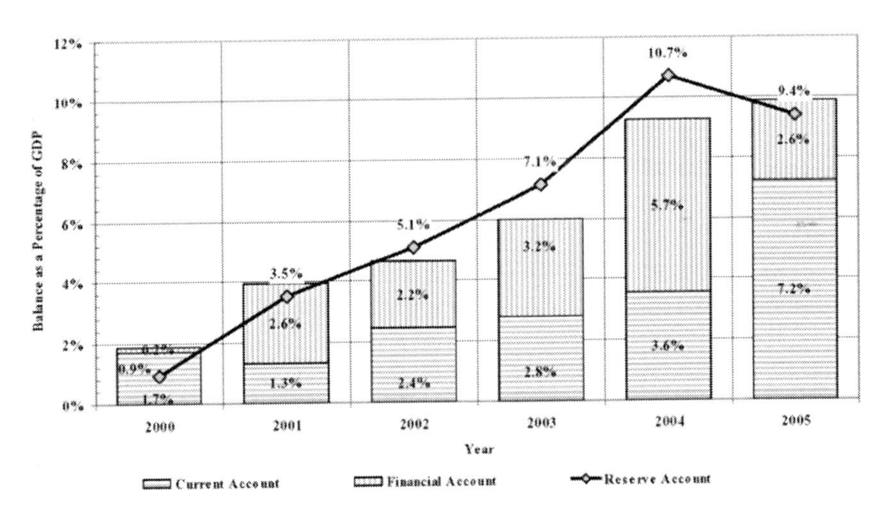

Graph 23. The People's Bank of China's Intervention in Foreign Exchange Market Drives External Imbalances, 2000-2005

Graph 23 shows how the interventions of the People's Bank of China drive the PRC's external imbalances. In the absence of official intervention, the sign on the current account balance and the financial account balance should be opposite. However, during the last six years, the PRC has run both current account surpluses (in horizontal stripe) and financial account surpluses (in vertical stripe). Official intervention through the reserve account (as represented by the solid black line with diamonds) has made current account and financial account surpluses possible simultaneously.

A. Underconsumption and Dependency on Export-Led Growth

Chinese farmers are notoriously inefficient. The average productivity of a Chinese farmer is one-sixteenth of the average productivity of other Chinese workers. This widening productivity gap is increase income inequality between urban and rural areas in the PRC. The OECD reported that the average income of urban workers was three times the average income of rural workers.[60]

Chinese farmers may lease agricultural land from local governments for up to 30 years.[61] Unlike residential, commercial, or industrial lessees, however, agricultural lessees may not mortgage or transfer their leases. Moreover, a survey found that only 13 percent of agricultural leases forbid local officials from reallocating land during the term of a lease.[62] If agricultural lessees were to stop farming and move to a city, they would forfeit their leases, and their land would be redistributed to other farmers.[63] Consequently, Chinese farmers have neither the ability nor the incentive to invest in fixed assets that would improve their productivity and increase their income.

Under its accession agreement with the World Trade Organization, the PRC agreed to open its domestic market to agricultural imports. If the renminbi were to appreciate rapidly and substantially, many Chinese farmers would not be able to compete with cheaper agricultural imports and would cease farming.

Because millions of Chinese are still employed in agriculture, currency appreciation could trigger mass unemployment and political instability in rural areas. On May 16, 2006, *Business Week* reported:

"To the Chinese government, the agricultural industry and small farm villages are the biggest political issue," says former Japanese financial diplomat Eisuke Sakakibara.[64]

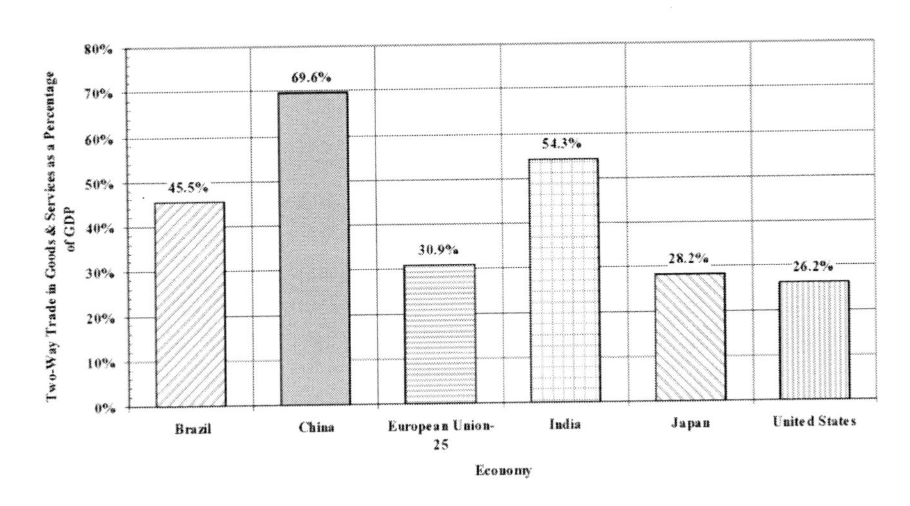

Graph 24. Two-Way Trade in Goods & Services as a Percentage of GDP in Major Populous Economies, 2005

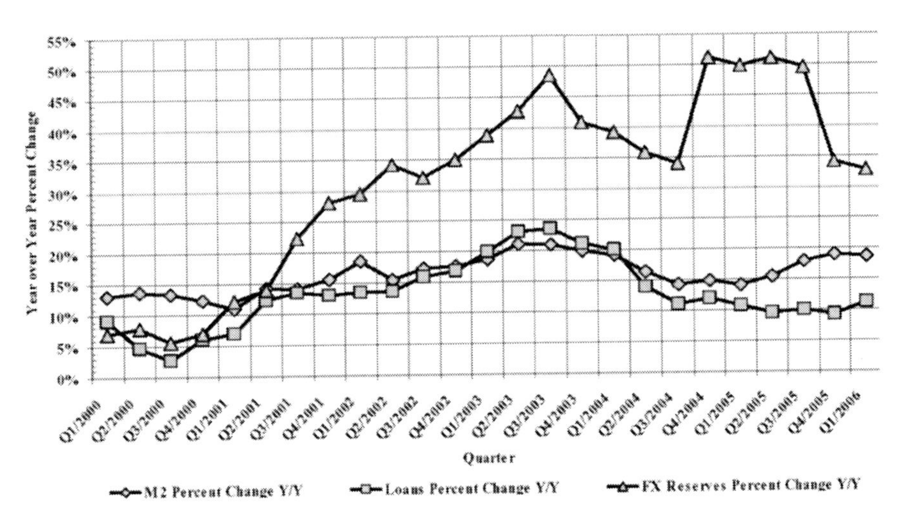

Graph 25. Year over Year Percent Changes in M2, Loans, and Foreign Exchange Reserves, Q1/2000 - Q1/2006

Under the “harmonious society” policy, President Hu Jintao is trying to increase rural income and provide alternative employment for displaced farmers by abolishing the twothousand-year-old agricultural tax, expanding micro-financing for starting small businesses, and investing in mega-projects in rural areas. Consequently, Hu wants the renminbi to appreciate very slowly until the benefits of these measures become apparent.

However, this exchange rate policy creates profound imbalances in the rest of the PRC’s economy. Intervention reduces the real incomes of Chinese workers and their consumption of imported goods and services. Consequently, the PRC cannot rely on domestic consumption to drive its economic expansion. The PRC remains overly dependent on exports and investment for economic growth. Consequently, the PRC’s two-way trade as a percent of its GDP is far higher than other populous economies (see Graph 24).

B. Overinvestment and Malinvestment

While the People’s Bank of China has tried to sterilize its interventions, the International Monetary Fund reported that China was only able to mop-up about half of the excess liquidity through bond sales. The remainder of this excess liquidity has contributed to rapid growth in both M2 and loans since 2000. The International Monetary Fund noted that the loan growth would have been even higher without the administrative interventions of the People’s Bank of China and the China Banking Regulatory Commission (see Graph 25).

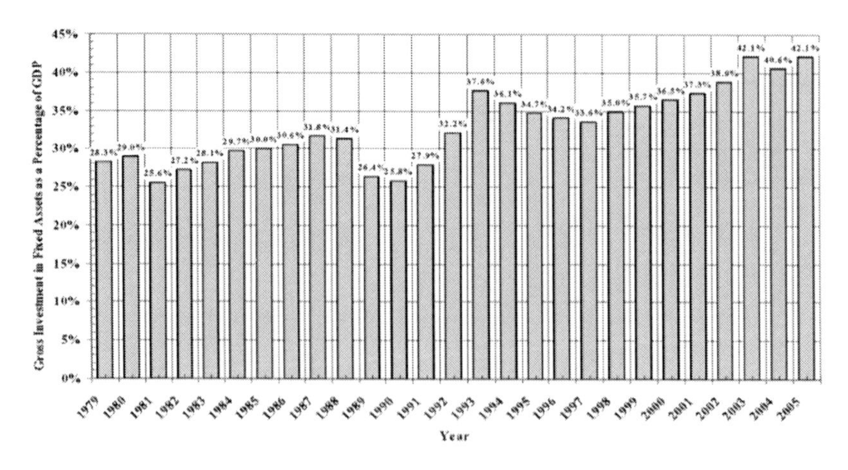

Graph 26. The PRC's Rate of Gross Investment in Fixed Assets, 1979-2005

The combination of (1) excessive liquidity from interventions that has not been fully sterilized and (2) *guanxi* loans and policy loans extended by Chinese banks has channeled funds to SOEs and SIEs, which invest in fixed assets. This aggressive lending helped to boost the PRC's rate of gross investment in fixed assets to 42.1 percent of GDP in 2005 (see Graph 26).[65] The PRC's gross investment rate is far higher than other major economies (see Graph 27).

Although the PRC's non-market allocation of financing may boost production and investment in the short term, the PRC's economic growth is sustainable over the long term if, and only if, firms:

- produce goods and services that the market demands; and
- invest in fixed assets that have a positive net present value.[66]

The rapid accumulation of fixed assets by the SOEs and the SIEs suggests that overinvestment (i.e., the acquisition of too many fixed assets for producing goods and services given expected future demand) and malinvestment (i.e., the acquisition of the wrong types of fixed assets for producing goods and services to meet expected future demand) may be occurring in the PRC. According to the *Economist Intelligence Unit*, "Oversupply has driven down prices in many industries, such as vehicles, steel, and aluminum."[67] Moreover, the *Economist Intelligence Unit* reported:

> *Government officials have long warned of oversupply in the [steel] sector, and in December 2005 the head of the National Development and Reform Commission, Ma Kai, declared that oversupply had led steel prices to decline to 2003 levels, with the prices of some steel products falling below cost. (This was a serious admission for a Chinese official, as it could pave the way for anti-dumping suits in China's steel export markets.)*[68]

An economic boom caused by overinvestment and malinvestment is not sustainable. The inevitable liquidation of overinvestment and malinvestment could cause a recession in the PRC and slow economic growth in the rest of the world.

To keep the renminbi undervalued, the People's Bank of China exchanges yuan for the U.S. dollars that the PRC's current and financial account surpluses pump into the Chinese economy. This intervention leaves Chinese banks and other depository institutions flush with cash. To remain profitable, Chinese banks are lending their excess deposits.

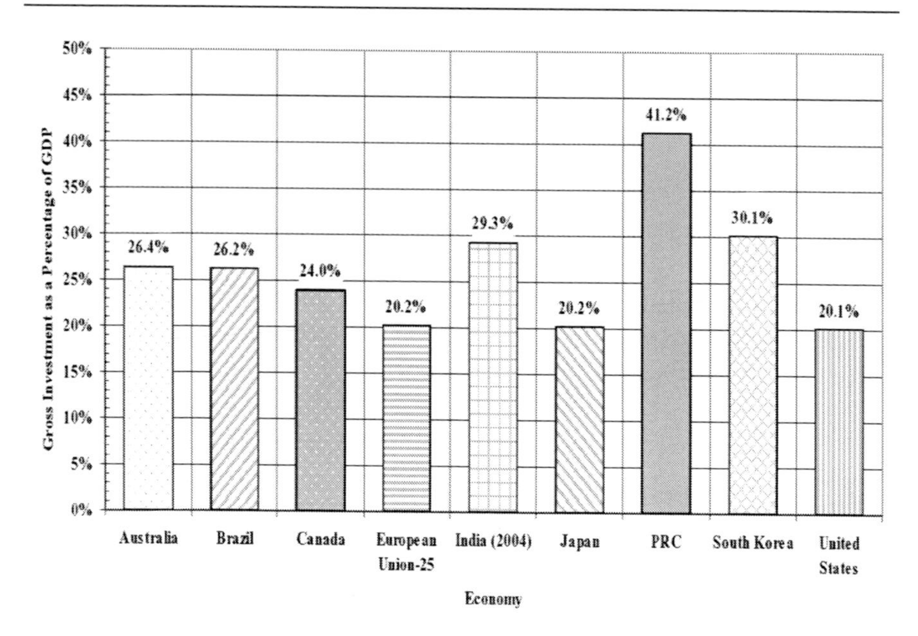

Graph 27. The PRC's Rate of Gross Investment in Fixed Assets is Unusually High Compared to Other Major Economies, 2005

Senior PRC officials are clearly concerned that the excessive lending is fueling an overinvestment and malinvestment bubble. Fearing that higher interest rates would attract more foreign capital, the People's Bank of China is reluctant to increase interest rates significantly to curb the rapid growth of domestic bank loans and the resulting inflation of an investment bubble. Instead, senior officials are relying on moral suasion and regulatory changes to moderate loan growth. On June 16, 2006, the *Financial Times* reported that the State Council had issued a series of edicts intended to curb the rapid growth of bank lending and new investments in real estate development. The article observed:

> *The root cause of the liquidity bubble, say economists, is China's managed currency, which has only appreciated by about 3 percent against the dollar since last July's decision to end a decade-long peg to the greenback.*[69]

Without a significant appreciation in the renminbi, private economists doubt that such administrative measures will have a significant effect.

C. International Imbalances

Because other developing Asian economies have labor-intensive industries and assembly operations that compete with the PRC, central banks in these economies fear that currency appreciation would put local firms or local subsidiaries of foreign multinational firms at a competitive disadvantage against Chinese firms or Chinese subsidiaries of foreign multinational firms. Thus, other developing Asian economies have mimicked the PRC's exchange rate policy (see Graph 28).

The People's Bank of China and central banks in other developing Asian economies use their accumulated foreign exchange to buy foreign debt securities, mainly U.S. Treasuries and Agencies, creating a non-market financial inflow into the United States. Given the accounting relationship between the current account and the capital and financial accounts, this non-market financial inflow increases the foreign exchange value of the U.S. dollar, the U.S. current account deficit, and the U.S. financial account surplus above market-determined levels. According to some economists, if the PRC and other developing Asian economies were to float their currencies, the U.S. current account deficit could decline by up to 10 percent.[70]

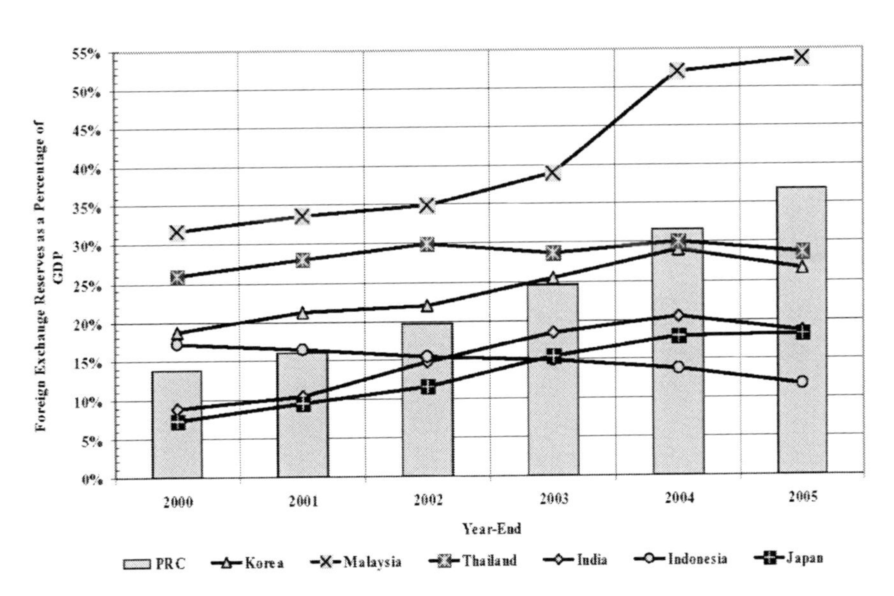

Graph 28. Foreign Exchange Reserves as a Percentage of GDP in Asian Economies, Year-End 2000-2005

IX. ANALYSIS

The PRC's current policies may not support a long-term continuation of the rapid growth that the Chinese economy has enjoyed in recent years. Because of the growing size of the Chinese economy and its deep integration through investment and trade flows with the rest of the world, a recession in the PRC would have adverse effects on the global economy.

The CPC's desire to retain power drove economic reform and shaped its contours. Senior officials are well aware that the PRC confronts a number of interrelated challenges to continued economic growth:

- A smaller working-age population will reduce China's labor supply. The combination of a higher labor demand and a smaller labor supply will inevitably increase the real compensation for all Chinese workers. Consequently, the PRC's current comparative advantage of low-cost labor will erode. The PRC will begin to shed many of the low-wage jobs in labor-intensive manufacturing and assembly operations that it has gained. To sustain economic growth and create high-wage replacement jobs, the PRC must climb the development ladder.
- The PRC currently faces a shortage of professionals and highly skilled workers. To alleviate this shortage, the PRC has increased the number of colleges and universities by 61.0 percent from 1,075 in 1990 to 1,731 in 2004 and quadrupled the number of students in post-secondary education.[71] However, this rapid expansion in the number of students appears to have undermined the quality of the post-secondary education that many students are receiving. Only about 10 percent of Chinese graduates receiving engineering degrees, for example, possess the minimum skills necessary for employment with U.S. engineering firms.[72] As the PRC begins to climb the development ladder, the demand for professionals and highly skilled workers will increase dramatically. The quality problems with the Chinese workforce may decelerate the PRC's economic growth rate.
- Corruption and the weak protection of intellectual property rights may retard the development of Chinese firms in creative industries that would help the PRC climb the development ladder.
- The PRC's rapidly aging population poses additional problems. The lack of a social safety net, along with the limited availability of private retirement plans, consumer credit, and insurance products,

drive Chinese households to save prodigiously. The resulting extraordinarily high gross saving rate hampers the PRC's ability to transition from export-led to domestic consumption-driven growth.

- SOEs and SIEs are generally inefficient. Many financially distressed SOEs and SIEs need large subsidies to survive. *Guanxi* loans and policy loans to subsidize financial distressed SOEs and SIEs have been a major cause of the nonperforming loan problem in Chinese banks and other depository institutions. *Guanxi* loans have also encouraged SOEs and SIEs to invest heavily in construction and real estate development. Many of these investments are speculative. A tidal wave of new nonperforming loans in Chinese banks and other depository institutions may now be forming.
- Non-market lending to SOEs and SIEs reduces the amount of credit available to Chinese households and private businesses, lowers the PRC's potential growth rate, and hinders the PRC's transition from export-led to domestic consumption- driven growth.
- An undervalued renminbi creates excess liquidity in state-influenced Chinese banks and other depository institutions. Excess liquidity encourages bankers to lend aggressively. In turn, easy credit encourages SOEs and SIEs that are insulated from price signals and profitability constraints to make speculative investments in fixed assets. The nexus among an undervalued exchange rate, state-influenced Chinese banks, and SOEs and SIEs is apparently creating widespread overinvestment and malinvestment in the PRC. This is especially true in the real estate sector. Such an investment bubble is unsustainable over the long term.
- An undervalued renminbi also fans protectionist sentiment abroad. Protectionism is particularly dangerous for the PRC, whose economic growth has been extraordinarily dependent on exports and foreign direct investment.
- The absence of secure and transferable property rights in agricultural land and the limited availability of credit inhibit Chinese farmers from making the investments in fixed assets necessary to increase low agricultural productivity and raise rural incomes. The wide and growing income gap between rural and urban China is fueling social tensions. Because inefficient Chinese farmers cannot compete with cheaper agricultural imports if the foreign exchange value of the renminbi were to increase substantially, senior officials have resisted any substantial increase in the foreign exchange value of the renminbi.

> However, this official reluctance is simultaneously inflating an investment bubble domestically and creating unsustainable imbalances internationally, which together threaten the PRC's rapid economic growth.

Senior officials fear that comprehensive reforms to resolve these interrelated challenges would cause significant economic dislocations and increase unemployment and political unrest in the short run and could weaken the CPC's sway over the Chinese economy in the long run. Consequently, senior officials have responded with incremental policy changes. However, the PRC may be reaching the limits of the effectiveness of its incremental approach to reform.

The PRC must begin to climb the development ladder as Japan, South Korea, and Singapore have done and southeast Asian economies such as Malaysia and Thailand are doing. The distortions from an undervalued exchange rate, non-market lending, overinvestment, and malinvestment – particularly by the SOEs and SIEs and in the real estate sector – are interrelated. The economic imbalances created by these distortions, along with rising disgust at widespread corruption, are fueling social unrest, especially in rural China. Consequently, a more comprehensive approach to solving these problems is needed.

To quell social unrest, the PRC must curb corruption, strengthen the rule of law, and narrow the productivity and income gaps between workers in rural and urban China. To avoid a nasty recession, the PRC must begin to reduce some of the growing imbalances in its economy. Simultaneous reforms of the PRC's agricultural land policies, its financial services sector, and its foreign exchange rate regime are necessary to resolve these festering problems and sustain rapid economic growth.

X. Conclusion

Although the Chinese economy is booming, the PRC faces five major challenges to sustain rapid economic growth in the future:

- unfavorable demographics;
- corruption and a weak rule of law;
- financially distressed SOEs and SIEs;

- a dysfunctional financial system; and
- domestic and international imbalances.

The PRC's response to these challenges will, of course, determine the future performance of the Chinese economy. However, since the Chinese economy is so large and well integrated into the global economy, the performance of the Chinese economy will also affect the performance of the United States and other economies in the world.

So far, the PRC's approach to reform has been incremental. This incremental approach may be reaching the limits of its effectiveness. The challenges that the PRC now faces are deeply interrelated. A more comprehensive approach to reform is needed.

End Notes

[1] On May 16, 1966, Chairman Mao Zedong launched the Great Proletarian Cultural Revolution to regain some of the political power that he had lost to CPC rivals after the economic disaster of the Great Leap Forward. During the next two years, Mao's wife, Jiang Qing, and other supporters organized the Red Guards to seize control of party organizations and government organs. Because of this power struggle, millions of Chinese died, were imprisoned, or were injured. Although Mao officially terminated the Cultural Revolution in 1969, historians date the end of the Cultural Revolution to the arrest of the Gang of Four (i.e., Jiang Qing and three of her associates, Zhang Chunqiao, Yao Wenyuan, and Wang Hongwen) in 1976.

[2] China National Bureau of Statistics/Haver Analytics.

[3] [U]sing the World Bank's $1 per day income standard, the number of poor is estimated to have dropped from about 490 million to 88 million over the same period, a decline in poverty incidence from 49 percent in 1981 to 6.9 percent in 2002. World Bank, Shanghai Poverty Conference: Case Study Summary (2004).

[4] Excludes intra-European Union goods trade. Author's calculation based on International Monetary Fund/Haver Analytics data.

[5] International Monetary Fund/Haver Analytics.

[6] Excludes intra-European Union goods trade. Author's calculation based on International Monetary Fund/Haver Analytics data.

[7] Author's calculation based on International Monetary Fund/Haver Analytics data.

[8] The "city-state" economies of Hong Kong and Singapore are also heavily reliant on foreign direct investment.

[9] China National Bureau of Statistics/Haver Analytics.

[10] *OECD Economic Survey: China* (Paris: Organization for Economic Cooperation and Development, 2005): 133.

[11] China National Bureau of Statistics/Haver Analytics.

[12] United Nations Population Division, *World Populations Prospects: The 2004 Revision Population Database*, http://esa.un.org/unpp/p2k0data.asp.

[13] Peter Marsh, "Foreign Makers Find Advantages on More Familiar Turf," *Financial Times* (May 7, 2006).

[14] Tom Mitchell, "How China is Handling Cost Rises by Boosting Value," *Financial Times* (May 7, 2006).

[15] United Nations Population Division, *World Populations Prospects: The 2004 Revision Population Database*(2004). Found at: http://esa.un.org/unpp/p2k0data.asp.

[16] Author's calculation based on the United Nations Population Division data.

[17] Ibid.

[18] The PRC has a pay-as-you-go defined benefit old-age pension plan for urban workers in the formal sector. Employers pay a payroll tax equal to 20 percent of an employee's base wage or salary. Covered employees are eligible for an old-age pension of 20 percent of the average wage in their locality after (1) completing fifteen years of service and (2) reaching the age of 60 for men, 50 for woman in manual labor, and 55 for other women. In addition, employees must contribute an additional 8 percent of their base wage or salary to defined contribution plans, of which 5 percentage points goes to a government notional plan and 3 percentage points goes to individual accounts. Upon retirement, annuity payments from the government notional plan are based an employee's notional balance divided by 120. Urban workers in the informal sector, rural workers, and self-employed individuals are not eligible for any of these plans.

[19] Author's calculation based upon data from China National Bureau of Statistics/Haver Analytics.

[20] Central and subsidiary governments now publish proposed laws and regulations and provide time for public comments before enactment. Public hearings have caused officials to modify some proposed laws and regulations.

[21] *China in the Global Economy*, "Civil Service Reform in China" (Paris: Organization for Economic Cooperation and Development, 2005): 55-60.

[22] *Transparency International Corruptions Practices Index 2005*, found at http:// transparency. org.

[23] The family name of this Chinese economist is listed last, according to western fashion.

[24] Julie Chao, "China is Losing Battle with Corruption," *Milwaukee Journal Sentinel* (December 8, 2002).

[25] *China Economic Quarterly* (First Quarter 2005): 48.

[26] Found at: http://www.chinabalancesheet.com/Documents/Data Domestic Sociopolitical.PDF.

[27] Stephen Wyatt, "Privatization More Hype than Reality," *Australian Financial Review* (June 7, 2005).

[28] OECD Survey: 126.

[29] China National Bureau of Statistics/Haver Analytics.

[30] Ibid.

[31] Author's calculation based on data from China National Bureau of Statistics/Haver Analytics.

[32] Minxi Pei, "Politics Blamed for China's Trillion-Dollar Bad Debts," *The Australian* (May 9, 2006). Found at http://www.theaustralian.news.com/printpage/0,5942,19067992,00.html.

[33] OECD Survey: 86.

[34] OECD Survey: 105.

[35] OECD Survey: 102-104.

[36] OECD Survey: 42; author's calculation based on data from World Federation of Exchanges and U.S. Bureau of Economic Analysis/Haver Analytics.

[37] Author calculation based on data from China Securities Regulatory Commission/Haver Analytics, China National Bureau of Statistics/Haver Analytics, New York Stock Exchange and NASDAQ/Haver Analytics, and U.S. Bureau of Economic Analysis/Haver Analytics.

[38] Author's calculation based on data from the People's Bank of China/Haver Analytics, China National Bureau of Statistics/Haver Analytics, Federal Reserve Flow of Funds/Haver Analytics, and U.S. Bureau of Economic Analysis/Haver Analytics.

[39] Ibid.

[40] The twelve joint stock commercial banks are:

Bank of Communications

CITIC Bank

Everbright Bank

Evergrowing Bank
Hua Xia Bank
Guangdong Development Bank
Shenzhen Development Bank
China Merchants Bank
Shanghai and Pudong Development Bank
Industrial Bank
Minsheng Bank
Zheshang Bank

[41] Author's calculation based on data from People's Bank of China/Haver Analytics.

[42] *Guanxi* lending refers to loans that banks make to individuals, firms, organizations, or governments based on personal relationships between bank officers and borrowers. Under *guanxi* lending, banks grant borrowers larger loans, lower interest rates, or more favorable terms than banks would willingly grant to borrowers without a personal relationship.

[43] Policy lending refers to loans that banks make to individuals, firms, organizations, or governments based on government regulations or suasion rather than market criteria. Under policy lending, banks grant borrowers larger loans, lower interest rates, or more favorable terms than banks would willingly grant in the absence of government regulation or suasion.

[44] Author's calculation based on data from People's Bank of China/Haver Analytics. Allocation of commercial loans to SOEs and SIEs and to private firms based on Diana Farrell et al., *Putting China's Capital to Work: The Value of Financial System Reform* (McKinsey Global Institute, May 2006): 11.

[45] Ibid: 15.

[46] Ibid: 81.

[47] Ibid: 90-91.

[48] The PRC's central government established asset management companies to liquidate nonperforming loans. The PRC modeled their asset management companies on the Resolution Trust Corporation. Congress established the Resolution Trust Corporation in 1989 through the *Financial Institutions Reform, Recovery, and Enforcement Act*. The Resolution Trust Corporation liquidated the nonperforming loans and other assets of saving and loan associations that had been declared insolvent.

[49] Author's calculations based on data from China Banking Regulatory Commission/China National Bureau of Statistics/Haver Analytics.

[50] Charlene Chu, Lynda Lin, Kate Lin, and David Marshall, "China: Taking Stock of Banking System Nonperforming Loans," *Fitch Ratings* (May 30, 2006). Found at http://www.fitchratings.com/dtp/pdf2- 06/bchi3005.pdf.

[51] *Global Nonperforming Loan Report*, Ernst & Young (May 3, 2006): 14. Author's calculation of nonperforming loans as a percent of GDP.

[52] Elaine Kurtenbach, "Ernst & Young Nixes Report Putting China's Potential Nonperforming Loans at US$911 Billion," *Financial Times* (May 15, 2006). Found at http://search.ft.com/searchArticle?id=060515009128&query=Ernst+%26+Young+China&vsc_appId=powerSearch&offset=0&resultsToShow=10&vsc_subjectConcept=&vsc_company Concept=&state=More&vsc_publicationGroups=TOPWFT&searchCat=-1.

[53] Charlene Chu, Lynda Lin, Kate Lin, and David Marshall, "China: Taking Stock of Banking System Nonperforming Loans," *Fitch Ratings* (May 30, 2006). Found at http://www.fitchratings.com/dtp/pdf2- 06/bchi3005.pdf.

[54] Brian Bremner, "China: Big Economy, Bigger Peril?" *Business Week* (June 13, 2006). Found at: http://www.businessweek.com/globalbiz/content/jun2006/gb20060613 168050.htm.

[55] *Economist Intelligence Unit* (2006): 30.

[56] In the United States, "dollar" is both the name of the U.S. currency and of its unit of account. In the People's Republic of China, the "renminbi" is the name of the PRC's currency, and "yuan" is the name of the PRC's unit of account.

[57] Equivalently, the U.S. dollar has depreciated by only 3.44 percent against the renminbi (from $1 equal to 8.2765 yuan on July 21, 2005, to $1 equal to 7.9918 yuan on July 20, 2006). Federal Reserve Bank of New York/Haver Analytics.

[58] People's Bank of China, State Administration of Foreign Exchange, and China National Bureau of Statistics /Haver Analytics.

[59] Morris Goldstein, *Renminbi Controversies*, Prepared for the Conference on Monetary Institutions and Economic Development, Cato Institute, November 3, 2005, revised December 2005): 1-4.

[60] OECD Survey: 44-45.

[61] The implementation of 30-year leasing is not universal and varies widely both among and within provinces. A survey found that only one-third of the villages in eleven provinces had implemented 30-year leasing. In the remaining villages, half of the agricultural land was leased on a long-term basis, while the remainder was leased through annual actions. OECD Survey: 113.

[62] OECD Survey: 113.

[63] In some cases, farmers may change their residential registration to a nearby village without losing their leases. However, these lessees may be required to pay additional fees to their local government to retain their leases. OECD Survey: 113.

[64] Brian Bremner, "Controlling China's Runaway Growth," *Business Week* (May 16, 2006). Found at: http://www.businessweek.com/globalbiz/content/may2006/gb20060516 457180.htm

[65] Author's calculations based on data from China National Bureau of Statistics/Haver Analytics.

[66] Net present value is the expected future revenues from an investment discounted by a rate that reflects the real interest rate, expected future inflation, and the risk associated with such investment less the current and future costs (also discounted) associated with the same investment.

[67] *Economist Intelligence Unit* (2006): 25.

[68] *Economist Intelligence Unit* (March 2006): 25-26.

[69] Richard McGregor, "Beijing Reins in Lending in Bid to Cool Growth," *Financial Times* (June 16, 2006).

[70] C. Fred Bergsten, "Clash of the Titans," *Newsweek* (international edition), April 24, 2006.

[71] *Economist Intelligence Unit* (March 2005): 20.

[72] Guy de Jonquieres, "The Critical Skills Gap," *Financial Times* (June 12, 2006).

In: The Chinese Economy
Editors: Benjamin A. Tyler pp.41-54
ISBN: 978-1-60876-937-7

Chapter 2

CHINA'S CURRENCY: A SUMMARY OF THE ECONOMIC ISSUES

Wayne M. Morrison and Marc Labonte

SUMMARY

Many Members of Congress charge that China's policy of accumulating foreign reserves (especially U.S. dollars) to influence the value of its currency constitutes a form of currency manipulation intended to make its exports cheaper and imports into China more expensive than they would be under free market conditions. They further contend that this policy has caused a surge in the U.S. trade deficit with China in recent years and has been a major factor in the loss of U.S. manufacturing jobs. Although China made modest reforms to its currency policy in 2005, resulting in a gradual appreciation of its currency (about 19% through June 3, 2009), many Members contend the reforms have not gone far enough and have warned of potential punitive legislative action. Although an undervalued Chinese currency has likely hurt some sectors of the U.S. economy, it has benefited others. For example, U.S. consumers have gained from the supply of low-cost Chinese goods (which helps to control inflation), as have U.S. firms using Chinesemade parts and materials (which helps such firms become more globally competitive). In addition, China has used its abundant foreign exchange reserves to buy U.S. securities, including U.S. Treasury securities, which are used to help fund the Federal budget deficit. Such purchases help keep U.S. interest rates relatively low. For China, an undervalued valued currency has boosted exports and attracted foreign investment, but has lead to unbalanced economic growth and suppressed Chinese living standards.

The current global economic crisis has further complicated the currency issue for both the United States and China. Although China is under pressure from the United States to appreciate its currency, it is reluctant to do so because that could cause further damage to export sector and lead to more layoffs. China has halted its gradual appreciation of its currency, the renminbi (RMB) or yuan to the dollar in 2009, keeping it relatively constant at about 6.83 yuan per dollar. The federal budget deficit has increased rapidly since FY2008, causing a sharp increase in the amount of Treasury securities that must be sold. The Obama Administration has encouraged China to continue purchasing U.S. debt. However, if China were induced to further appreciate its currency against the dollar, it could slow its accumulation of foreign exchange reserves, thus reducing the need to invest in dollar assets, such as Treasury securities. Legislation has been introduced in the 111th Congress to address China's currency policy.

China's currency policy appears to have created a policy dilemma for the Chinese government. A strong and stable U.S. economy is in China's national interest since the United States is China's largest export market. Thus, some analysts contend that China will feel compelled to keep funding the growing U.S. debt. However, Chinese officials have expressed concern that the growing U.S. debt will eventually spark inflation in the United States and a depreciation of the dollar, which would negatively impact the value of China's holdings of U.S. securities. But if China stopped buying U.S. debt or tried to sell off a large portion of those holdings, it could also cause the dollar to depreciate and thus reduce the value of its remaining holdings, and such a move could further destabilize the U.S. economy. Chinese concerns over its large dollar holdings appear to have been reflected in a paper issued by the governor of the People's Bank of China, Zhou Xiaochuan on March 24, 2009, which called for replacing the U.S. dollar as the international reserve currency with a new global system controlled by the International Monetary Fund. China has also signed currency swap agreements with six of its trading partners, which would allow those partners to settle accounts with China using the yuan rather than the dollar.

INTRODUCTION

From 1994 until July 2005, China maintained a policy of pegging its currency, the renminbi (RMB) or yuan, to the U.S. dollar at an exchange rate of roughly 8.28 yuan to the dollar.[1] The Chinese central bank maintained this peg by buying (or selling) as many dollar-denominated assets in exchange for newly printed yuan as needed to eliminate excess demand (supply) for the yuan. As a result, the exchange rate between the yuan and the dollar basically stayed the same, despite changing economic factors which could have otherwise caused the yuan to either appreciate or depreciate relative to the dollar. Under a floating exchange rate system, the relative demand for the two countries' goods and assets would determine the exchange rate of the yuan to the dollar. Many economists contend that for the first several years of the peg, the fixed value was likely close to the market value. But in the past few years, economic conditions have changed such that the yuan would likely have appreciated if it had been floating. The sharp increase in China's foreign exchange reserves (which grew from $403 billion in 2003 to $1.95 trillion as of March 2009) and China's large trade surplus with the world ($297 billion in 2008) are often viewed by critics of China's currency policy as proof that the yuan is significantly undervalued.

CHINA REFORMS THE PEG

The Chinese government modified its currency policy on July 21, 2005. It announced that the yuan's exchange rate would become "adjustable, based on market supply and demand with reference to exchange rate movements of currencies in a basket" (it was later announced that the composition of the basket includes the dollar, the yen, the euro, and a few other currencies) and that the exchange rate of the U.S. dollar against the yuan was adjusted from 8.28 to 8.11, an appreciation of 2.1%. Unlike a true floating exchange rate, the yuan would be allowed to fluctuate by up to 0.3% (later changed to 0.5%) on a daily basis against the basket.

Since July 2005, China has allowed the yuan to appreciate steadily, but very slowly. It has continued to accumulate foreign reserves at a rapid pace, which suggests that if the yuan were allowed to freely float it would appreciate much more rapidly. The current situation might be best described as a "managed float"—market forces are determining the general direction of the yuan's movement, but the government is retarding its rate of appreciation through market intervention. From July 21, 2005 to April 13, 2009, the dollar-yuan exchange rate went from 8.11 to 6.83, an appreciation of 18.7%. The effects of the yuan's appreciation are unclear. The price index for U.S. imports from China in 2008, rose by 3.0% (compared to a 0.9% rise in import prices for total U.S. imports of non-petroleum products).[2] In 2008, U.S. imports from China rose by 5.1% over the previous year, compared to import growth of 11.7% in 2007; however, U.S. exports over this period were up 9.5% compared with an 18.1% rise in 2007. The current global economic slowdown appears to have sharply reduced bilateral trade. During the first three months of 2009, U.S. exports to, and imports from, China were down by 20% and 11%, respectively.

U.S. Concerns Over China's Currency Policy

Many U.S. policymakers and business and labor representatives have charged that China's currency is significantly undervalued vis-à-vis the U.S. dollar (even after the recent revaluation), making Chinese exports to the United States cheaper, and U.S. exports to China more expensive, than they would be if exchange rates were determined by market forces. They further argue that the undervalued currency has contributed to the burgeoning U.S. trade deficit with China (which was $266 billion in 2008) and has hurt U.S. production and employment in several U.S. manufacturing sectors that are forced to compete domestically and internationally against "artificially" low-cost goods from China. Furthermore, some analysts contend that China's currency policy induces other East Asian countries to intervene in currency markets in order to keep their currencies weak against the dollar in order to compete with Chinese goods. Critics contend that, while it may have been appropriate for China during the early stages of its economic development to maintain a pegged currency, it should let the yuan freely float today, given the size of the Chinese economy and the impact its policies have on the world economy.

CHINA'S CONCERNS OVER MODIFYING ITS CURRENCY POLICY

Chinese officials argue that its currency policy is not meant to favor exports over imports, but instead to foster economic stability through currency stability, as many other countries do. They have expressed concern that floating its currency could spark an economic crisis in China and would especially be damaging to its export industries at a time when painful economic reforms (such as closing down inefficient state-owned enterprises) are being implemented. They further contend that the Chinese banking system is too underdeveloped and burdened with heavy debt to be able to deal effectively with possible speculative pressures that could occur with a fully convertible currency. The global financial crisis has had a significant impact on China's trade and foreign direct investment (FDI) flows. China's trade (exports and imports) and inflows of FDI declined each month from November 2008 to April 2009 on a year-on-year basis. In February 2009, China's exports and imports were down 25.7% and 24.1%, respectively (year-on-year basis), the biggest monthly decline recorded since reforms began in 2009.[3] Thousands of export-oriented factories have reportedly been shut down. The Chinese government has estimated that 20 million migrant workers lost their jobs because of the global financial crisis in 2008. Chinese officials view economic stability as critical to sustaining political stability; they fear an appreciated currency could cause even more employment disruptions and thus could cause worker unrest. However, Chinese officials have indicated that their long-term goal is to adopt a more flexible exchange rate system and to seek more balanced economic growth through increased domestic consumption and the development of rural areas, but they claim they want to proceed at a gradual pace.

IMPLICATIONS OF CHINA'S CURRENCY POLICY FOR ITS ECONOMY

If the yuan is undervalued vis-à-vis the dollar (estimates rage from 15% to 40% or higher), then Chinese exports to the United States are likely cheaper than they would be if the currency were freely traded, providing a boost to China's export industries (and, to some degree, an indirect subsidy). Eliminating exchange rate risk through a managed peg also increases the attractiveness of China as a destination for foreign investment in export-oriented production facilities. However, an undervalued currency makes imports more expensive, hurting Chinese consumers and Chinese firms that import parts, machinery, and raw materials. Such a policy, in effect, benefits Chinese exporting firms (many of which are owned by foreign multinational corporations) at the expense of non-exporting Chinese firms, especially those that rely on imported goods. This may impede the most efficient allocation of resources in the Chinese economy. Another major problem is that the Chinese government must expand the money supply in order to keep purchasing dollars, which has promoted the banks to adopt easy credit policies.[4] In addition, in the past, "hot money" has poured into China from investors speculating that China will continue to appreciate the yuan. At some point, these factors could help fuel inflation, overinvestment in various sectors, and expansion of nonperforming loans by the banks—each of which could threaten future economic growth.

IMPLICATIONS OF CHINA'S CURRENCY POLICY FOR THE U.S. ECONOMY

Effect on Exporters and Import-Competitors

When exchange rate policy causes the yuan to be less expensive than it would be if it were determined by supply and demand, it causes Chinese exports to be relatively inexpensive and U.S. exports to China to be relatively expensive. As a result, U.S. exports and the production of U.S. goods and services that compete with Chinese imports fall, in the short run.[5] Many of the affected firms are in the manufacturing sector.[6] This causes the trade deficit to rise and reduces aggregate demand in the short run, all else equal.[7] Some analysts contend that China's currency policy constitutes a de facto or indirect export subsidy and should be subject to U.S. countervailing laws.

Effect on U.S. Consumers and Certain Producers

A society's economic well-being is usually measured not by how much it can produce, but how much it can consume. An undervalued yuan that lowers the price of imports from China allows the United States to increase its consumption through an improvement in the terms-of-trade. Since changes in aggregate spending are only temporary, from a long-term perspective the lasting effect of an undervalued yuan is to increase the purchasing power of U.S. consumers. Imports from China are not limited to consumption goods. U.S. producers also import capital equipment and inputs to final products from China. An undervalued yuan lowers the price of these U.S. products, increasing their output.

Effect on U.S. Borrowers

An undervalued yuan also has an effect on U.S. borrowers. When the U.S. runs a current account deficit with China, an equivalent amount of capital flows from China to the United States, as can be seen in the U.S. balance of payments accounts. This occurs because the Chinese central bank or private Chinese citizens are investing in U.S. assets, which allows more U.S. capital investment in plant and equipment to take place than would otherwise occur. Capital investment increases because the greater demand for U.S. assets puts downward pressure on U.S. interest rates, and firms are now willing to make investments that were previously unprofitable. This increases aggregate spending in the short run, all else equal, and also increases the size of the economy in the long run by increasing the capital stock.

Private firms are not the only beneficiaries of the lower interest rates caused by the capital inflow (trade deficit) from China. Interest-sensitive household spending, on goods such as consumer durables and housing, is also higher than it would be if capital from China did not flow into the United States. In addition, a large proportion of the U.S. assets bought by the Chinese, particularly by the central bank, are U.S. Treasury securities, which fund U.S. federal budget deficits. According to the U.S. Treasury Department, China held $$764 billion in U.S. Treasury securities as of April 2009, making it the largest foreign holder of such securities. If the U.S. trade deficit with China were eliminated, Chinese capital would no longer flow into this country on net, and the government would have to find other buyers of U.S. Treasuries. This could increase the government's interest payments.

Net Effect on the U.S. Economy

In the medium run, an undervalued yuan neither increases nor decreases aggregate demand in the United States. Rather, it leads to a compositional shift in U.S. production, away from U.S. exporters and import-competing firms toward the firms that benefit from Chinese capital flows. Thus, it is expected to have no medium or long run effect on aggregate U.S. employment or unemployment. As evidence, one can consider that the U.S. had a historically large and growing trade deficit throughout the 1990s at a time when unemployment reached a three-decade low. However, the gains and losses in employment and production caused by the trade deficit will not be dispersed evenly across regions and sectors of the economy: on balance, some areas will gain while others will lose. And by shifting the composition of U.S. output to a higher capital base, the size of the economy would be larger in the long run as a result of the capital inflow/trade deficit.

Although the compositional shift in output has no negative effect on aggregate U.S. output and employment in the long run, there may be adverse short-run consequences. If output in the trade sector falls more quickly than the output of U.S. recipients of Chinese capital rises, aggregate spending and employment could temporarily fall. This is more likely to be a concern if the economy is already sluggish than if it is at full employment. Otherwise, it is likely that government macroeconomic policy adjustment and market forces can quickly compensate for any decline of output in the trade sector by expanding other elements of aggregate demand. The deficit with China has not prevented the U.S. economy from registering high rates of growth.

The U.S.-China Trade Deficit in the Context of the Overall U.S. Trade Deficit

While China is a large trading partner, it accounted for only 16.1% of U.S. merchandise imports in 2008 and 33% of the sum of all U.S. bilateral trade deficits.[8] Over a span of several years, a country with a floating exchange rate can consistently run an overall trade deficit for only one reason: a domestic imbalance between saving and investment. Over the past two decades, U.S. saving as a share of gross domestic product (GDP) has been in gradual decline. On the one hand, the U.S. has high rates of productivity growth and strong economic fundamentals that are conducive to high rates of capital investment. On the other hand, it has a chronically low household saving rate, and recently a negative government saving rate as a result of the budget deficit. As long as Americans save little, foreigners will use their saving to finance profitable investment opportunities in the United States; the trade deficit is the result.[9] The returns to foreign-owned capital will flow to foreigners instead of Americans, but the returns to U.S. labor utilizing foreign-owned capital will flow to U.S. labor.

More than half of China's exports to the world are produced by foreign-invested firms in China, many of which have shifted production to China in order to gain access to low-cost labor. (The returns to capital of U.S. owned firms in China flow to Americans.) Such firms import raw materials and components (much of which come from East Asia) for assembly in China. As a result, China tends to run trade deficits with East Asian countries (such as Taiwan, South Korea, and Japan) and trade surpluses with countries with high consumer demand, such as the United States. These factors imply that much of the increase in U.S. imports (and hence, the rising trade deficit with China) is largely the result of China becoming a production platform for many foreign companies, rather than unfair Chinese trade policies.

THE GLOBAL FINANCIAL CRISIS AND CHINA'S CURRENCY

The impact of the global financial crisis has raised concerns in the United States over the future course of China's currency policy. Prior to the crisis, there were high expectations among many analysts that China would continue to appreciate its currency and implement financial reforms to pave the way towards eventually adopting a floating currency. However, China's economy has slowed significantly in recent months, due largely to a fall in global demand for Chinese products. The Chinese government appears to have halted the yuan's appreciation over the past few months. The rate of exchange between the yuan and the dollar on January 1, 2009 and June 3, 2009 stayed relatively constant 6.83 yuan per dollar, indicating that the Chinese government has, at least temporarily, halted its policy of allowing the yuan to gradually appreciate.

It is not known the extent to which the government is intervening to maintain the current exchange rate, and whether the government is buying dollars to limit appreciation, or selling dollars, to limit further devaluation.

Either way, a stable exchange rate with the dollar benefits China in a number of ways:

- **Exports and Foreign Direct Investment.** Keeping the exchange rate with the dollar stable may help to stem further declines in exports and FDI and thus halt further factory closings and layoffs in such sectors.

- **China as a "Responsible Stakeholder."** Over the past several years, Chinese leaders have sought to portray China as a responsible stakeholder (and increasingly a leader) on global economic issues. Chinese officials contend that during the 1997-98 Asian crisis, when several other nations sharply devalued their currencies, China "held the line" by not devaluing its currency, which might have prompted a new round of destructive devaluations across Asia. This policy was highly praised at the time by U.S. officials, including President Clinton. Although devaluing the RMB against the dollar could help China's trade sector, it could cause other economies in the Asia to devalue their currencies, which could further undermine economic stability in the region and negatively affect China's relations with its neighbors.

- **Avoiding Trade Tensions.** Chinese officials appear to be deeply concerned over "growing protectionism" in the United States. They are keenly aware that numerous congressional proposals have been introduced in the past which would take tough action against China's currency policy.

- **Protecting the Value of China's Investments.** China is believed to hold more than $1 trillion in U.S. securities. A major concern for Chinese officials as it has gradually appreciated the currency (until recently) has been the decline in value of these assets brought about by that appreciation. Thus, halting the appreciation of the yuan halts further losses from U.S.-held assets.

There may be a number of reasons why holding the exchange rate constant may not beneficial to China:

- **Continued Reliance on Exports and Fixed Investment**. Numerous economists contend that China needs to rebalance its economy by lessening its dependence on exports and fixed investment, which have been largely driven by China's currency policy, and do more to promote domestic consumption, improve the social safety net, and boost living standards among the poor. Such analysts contend that an appreciation of the yuan to "market levels" is a key factor to attaining a more balanced economy (by eliminating economic distortions caused by an undervalued currency).

- **Holding the Line May Not be Enough to Stop Congressional Action.** Although China allowed its currency to appreciate somewhat after 2005, it did not stem the tide of congressional criticism over its exchange rate policy. China has constantly argued that it has increasingly making its exchange rate system more flexible. Halting appreciation of the yuan may be viewed by some Members as an abandonment of China's commitments to reform the currency. Keeping the exchange rate with the dollar roughly the same could lessen the chance that such bills would be acted upon (see "Legislation," below).

- **The View That China Could Do More to Promote Global Recovery.** Chinese officials have stated that their biggest contribution to a global economic recovery is to maintain its rapid economic growth. To that end, the government is in the process of implementing a $586 billion stimulus plan (announced in November 2008), a large share of which will go into infrastructure projects. It is not clear to what extent the stimulus package will promote imports. Some analysts have contended that if China combined domestic spending with more market opening measures, including adopting a more flexible exchange rate policy, it would greatly boost China's imports. This would help stimulate economic recoveries in other countries, and also improve living standards in China.[10]

The Obama Administration has encouraged China to continue purchasing U.S. debt. Secretary of State Hillary Clinton was reportedly quoted as saying,

> Well, I certainly do think that the Chinese government and the central bank here in China is making a very smart decision by continuing to invest in treasury bonds for two reasons.... (Second,) the Chinese know that, in order to start exporting again to its biggest market, namely, the United States, the

> United States has to take some very drastic measures with this stimulus package, which means we have to incur more debt. It would not be in China's interest if we were unable to get our economy moving again. So, by continuing to support American Treasury instruments, the Chinese are recognizing our interconnection.[11]

China's currency policy appears to have created a policy dilemma for the Chinese government. A strong and stable U.S. economy is in China's national interest since the United States is China's largest export market. Thus, some analysts contend that China will feel compelled to keep funding the growing U.S. debt. However, Chinese officials have expressed concern that the growing U.S. debt will eventually spark inflation in the United States and a depreciation of the dollar, which would negatively impact the value of China's holdings of U.S. securities. But if China stopped buying U.S. debt or tried to sell off a large portion of those holdings, it could also cause the dollar to depreciate and thus reduce the value of its remaining holdings, and such a move could further destabilize the U.S. economy. Chinese concerns over its large dollar holdings appear to have been reflected in a paper issued by the governor of the People's Bank of China, Zhou Xiaochuan on March 24, 2009, which called for replacing the U.S. dollar as the international reserve currency with a new global system controlled by the International Monetary Fund.[12] China has also signed currency swap agreements totaling 650 billion yuan (or about $95 billion) with Hong Kong, Argentina, Indonesia, South Korea, Malaysia, and Belarus, which would allow those partners to settle accounts with China using the yuan rather than the dollar in order to facilitate bilateral trade and investment.[13] It is not clear if such a move signifies a gradual effort on the part of the Chinese government to eventually make the yuan an internationally traded currency.

Chinese data indicate that its accumulation of foreign exchange reserves has slowed sharply in 2009. From the end of December 2008 to the end of March 2009, those reserves grew by only $7.7 billion, reflecting sharp decreases in China's net exports, foreign direct investment, and hot money inflows (see Figure 1). If this trends continues, it will lessen China's need to intervene to keep the value of yuan against the dollar within its targeted range. However, it could also slow China's purchases of U.S. securities.[14] In fact, China's holdings of U.S. Treasury Securities fell by $4.4 billion in April 2009 over March 2009 holdings.

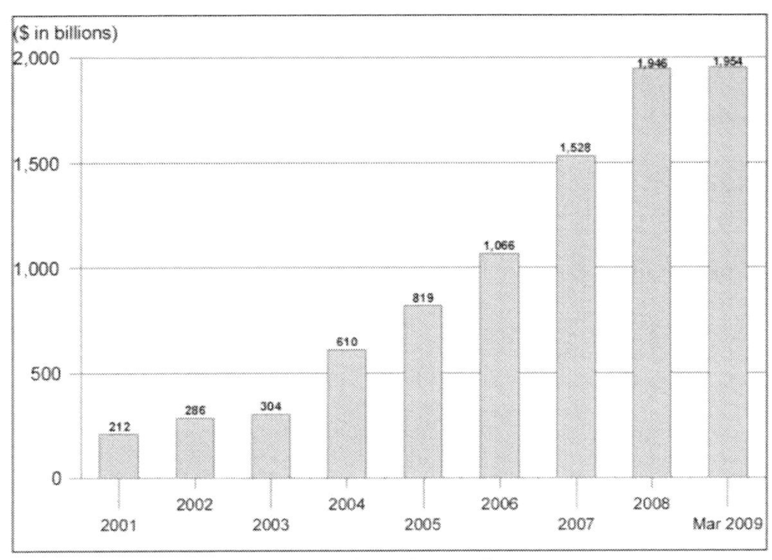

Source: Chinese State Administration of Foreign Exchange.
Note: End-year or end-month data.

Figure 1. China's Accumulation of Foreign Exchange Reserves: 2001-March 2009 $billions

Legislation

Numerous bills have been introduced over the past few years that seek to induce China to reform its currency. Bills in the 111th Congress include the following.

- H.R. 2378 (Tim Ryan) and S. 1027 (Stabenow) would make fundamental exchange-rate misalignment by any foreign nation actionable under U.S. countervailing laws (dealing with government subsidies and antidumping (dealing with products sold at fair market value).
- S. 1254 (Schumer) would require the Treasury Department to identify currencies that are fundamentally misaligned and to designate currencies for "priority action" under certain circumstances. Such action would include factoring currency undervaluation in U.S. anti-dumping cases, banning federal procurement of products or services

from the designated country, and filing a case against that country in the WTO.

End Notes

[1] The official name of China's currency is the renminbi (RMB), which is denominated in yuan units. Both RMB and yuan are used to describe China's currency.
[2] Bureau of Labor Statistics, *Import/Export Price Indexes,* Press Release, January 14, 2009.
[3] See CRS Report RS22984, *China and the Global Financial Crisis: Implications for the United States*, by Wayne M. Morrison
[4] Prior to the current global economic slowdown, easy monetary policies were contributing to inflationary pressures in China.
[5] Many such firms contend that China's currency policy constitutes one of several unfair trade advantages enjoyed by Chinese firms, including low wages, lack of enforcement of safety and environmental standards, selling below cost (dumping) and direct assistance from the Chinese government.
[6] U.S. production has moved away from manufacturing and toward the service sector over the past several years. U.S. employment in manufacturing as a share of total nonagricultural employment fell from 31.8% in 1960, to 22.4% in 1980, to 10.2% in 2007. This trend is much larger than the Chinese currency issue and is caused by numerous other factors.
[7] Putting exchange rate issues aside, most economists maintain that trade is a win-win situation for the economy as a whole, but produces losers within the economy. Economists generally argue that free trade should be pursued because the gains from trade are large enough that the losers from trade can be compensated by the winners, and the winners will still be better off.
[8] This figure is somewhat misleading because the United States run trade deficits with some countries and surpluses with others. A different approach would be to sum up the balances of those countries in which the United States ran a trade deficit with. In 2008, the United States ran trade deficits with 91 countries in 2008, totaling $951.9 billion; the U.S. trade deficit with China was equal to 27.9% of this amount
[9] Most economists believe that the United States runs a trade deficit because it fails to save enough to meet its investment needs and must obtain savings from other countries with high savings rates. China has one of the world's largest savings rate.
[10] Many Chinese have become increasing critical of China's currency policy because the large levels of foreign exchange reserves generated by that policy are invested in overseas assets with relatively low (and sometimes negative) returns.
[11] Secretary Clinton, Interview With Yang Lan of Dragon TV, Beijing, China, February 22, 2009.
[12] For copy of the proposal, see the Chinese People's Bank of China website at http://www.pbc.gov .cn/english/detail.asp?col=6500&id=178.
[13] Under a currency swap arrangement, two parties exchange currencies for a certain length of time and agree to reverse the transaction at a later date. See, the Federal Reserve Bank of New York, *the Basics of Foreign Trade and Exchange,* available at http://www.ny.frb.org/education/fx/foreign.html.
[14] See, CRS Report RL34314, *China's Holdings of U.S. Securities: Implications for the U.S. Economy,* by Wayne M. Morrison and Marc Labonte.

In: The Chinese Economy
Editors: Benjamin A. Tyler pp.55-84
ISBN: 978-1-60876-937-7

Chapter 3

CHINA'S ECONOMIC CONDITIONS

Wayne M. Morrison

SUMMARY

Since the initiation of economic reforms 30 years ago, China has become one of the world's fastest-growing economies. From 1979 to 2008 China's real gross domestic product (GDP) grew at an average annual rate of nearly 10%; it grew 13% in 2007 (the fastest annual growth since 1994). However, the current global economic crisis has hit China hard – real GDP growth slowed to 9% in 2008, and many analysts predict the economy will slow even more sharply in 2009. Millions of workers have reportedly already lost their jobs. This is of great concern to the Chinese government, which views healthy economic growth as critical to maintaining social stability. China also faces a number of other challenges to its economic growth and stability, including pervasive government corruption, an inefficient banking system, over-dependence on exports and fixed investment for growth, the lack of rule of law, severe pollution, and widening income disparities. The Chinese government has indicated that it intends to create a "harmonious society" over the coming years that would promote more balanced economic growth and address a number of economic and social issues. The severity of the current global economic crisis has induced the Chinese government to seek means to quickly promote greater domestic demand; in November the government announced plans to implement a $586 billion economic stimulus package, largely aimed at infrastructure projects.

Trade and foreign investment plays a major role in China's booming economy. From 2004 to 2008, the value of total Chinese merchandise trade doubled. It is estimated that in 2008 China was the world's second largest merchandise exporter and the third largest importer. Over half of China's trade is conducted by foreign-invested firms in China. In 2008, foreign direct investment (FDI) in China totaled $92 billion, making it the third largest global destination for FDI. The combination of large trade surpluses, FDI flows, and large-scale purchases of foreign currency have helped make China the world's largest holder of foreign exchange reserves at $1.9 trillion at the end 2008. The global financial crisis is having a significant impact on China's trade, as exports and imports in November and December 2008 and January 2009 declined on a year-onyear basis. FDI flows have also declined sharply during this period.

China's economy and its economic policies are of major concern to many U.S. policymakers. On the one hand, U.S. consumers, exporters, and investors have greatly benefitted from China's rapid economic and trade growth. China's large holdings of U.S. securities have helped keep U.S. interest rates relatively low. Many analysts hope that China will make positive contributions to a global economic recovery. On the other hand, the surge in U.S. imports of Chinese products has put competitive pressures on various U.S. industries. Many U.S. policymakers have argued that China maintains a number of economic policies that violate its commitments in the World Trade Organization and/or are harmful to U.S. economic interests, such as its currency policy. Concerns have also been raised over China's rising demand for energy and raw materials (and the impact of that demand has on world prices), increased pollution levels, China's growing FDI (such as in energy and raw materials) around the world, including countries where the United States has political and human rights concerns, and the potential implications of China's large holdings of U.S. debt. The global economic crisis has also raised concerns over the future pace of Chinese economic reforms. This chapter provides an overview of China's economic development, challenges China faces to maintain growth, and the implications of China's rise as a major economic power for the United States.

The rapid rise of China as a major economic power within a time span of about 30 years is often described by analysts as one of the greatest economic success stories in modern times. From 1979 (when economic reforms began) to 2008, China's real gross domestic product (GDP) grew at an average annual rate of nearly 10%. From 1980 to 2008, China's economy grew14 fold in real terms, and real per capita GDP (a common measurement of living standards) grew over 11 fold. By some measurements, China is now the world's second largest economy and some analysts predict it could become the largest within a few decades.

China's economic rise has led to a substantial increase in U.S.-China economic ties. Total trade between the two countries surged from $5 billion in 1980 to $409 billion in 2008 (U.S. data). In 2008, China was the United States's second largest trading partner, its third largest export market, and its largest source of imports. Many U.S. companies have extensive operations in China in order to sell their products in the booming Chinese market and to take advantage of low-cost labor for export-oriented manufacturing. These operations have helped U.S. firms remain internationally competitive and have supplied U.S. consumers with a variety of low-cost goods. China's large-scale purchases of U.S. Treasury securities have enabled the federal government to fund its budget deficits, which helps keep U.S. interest rates relatively low.

However, the emergence of China as a major economic superpower has raised concern among many U.S. policymakers. Some express concern over the large and growing U.S. trade deficits with China, which rose from $10 billion in 1990 to $266 billion in 2008, and are viewed by many Members of Congress as an indicator that U.S.-Chinese commercial relations are imbalanced or unfair. Others claim that China uses unfair trade practices (such as an undervalued currency and subsidies to domestic producers) to flood U.S. markets with low-cost goods, and that such practices threaten American jobs, wages, and living standards.

China faces a number of significant economic challenges, including the fallout from the global financial crisis (which has slowed foreign demand for its exports and hence threatens economic growth), a weak banking system, widening income gaps, growing pollution, unbalanced economic growth (through over-reliance on exports and fixed investment), and widespread economic efficiencies resulting from non-market policies. The Chinese government views a growing economy as vital to maintaining social stability.

This chapter provides background on China's economic rise and current economic structure and the challenges China faces to keep its economy growing strong, and describes Chinese economic policies that are of concern to U.S. policymakers.

MOST RECENT DEVELOPMENTS

- On March 5, 2009, the Bank of China reported that the exchange rate between China's currency (the renminbi or yuan) and the U.S. dollar stood at 6.84, an appreciation of about 19% since China's currency was reformed in July 2005.
- At a press conference during her visit to China on February 21, 2009, Secretary of State Hillary Rodham Clinton stated that she appreciated "greatly the Chinese government's continuing confidence in the United States treasuries."
- On February 16, 2009, the Chinese government stated that foreign direct investment (FDI) in China in January had declined 5.7% on a year-on-year basis. On February 11, the government reported that exports and imports had declined by 17.5% and 43.1%, respectively, on a year-on-year basis.
- On February 12, 2009, a Chinese state-owned firm, Aluminum Corporation of China (Chinalco), announced it would invest $19.5 billion in Rio Tinto Group (a leading international mining group), the largest Chinese overseas investment to date.
- On February 1, 2009, the Chinese government announced that 20 million migrant workers (15.4% out of an estimated 130 million migrants) had lost their jobs due to the global financial crisis.
- On November 15, 2008, Chinese President Hu Jintao attended the summit meeting of the Group of 20 (G-20) countries in Washington, D.C. to discuss the current global financial crisis. Hu stated that "steady and relatively fast growth in China is in itself an important contribution to international financial stability and world economic growth."
- On November 9, 2008, the Chinese government announced it would implement a two-year, $586 billion stimulus package, mainly dedicated to infrastructure projects.
- On June 13, 2008, the Netherlands Environmental Assessment Agency announced that, according to its estimates, China in 2007 became the world's largest emitter of CO_2, surpassing the United States by 14%, and accounting for two-thirds of last year's global carbon dioxide increase.
- On May 12, 2008, China's Sichuan Province was struck by a strong earthquake. The Chinese government estimated that (as of June 23,

2008) 69,181 people were killed, 374,171 injured, and 18,498 were missing.

An Overview of China's Economic Development

China's Economy Prior to Reforms

Prior to 1979, China maintained a centrally planned, or command, economy. A large share of the country's economic output was directed and controlled by the state, which set production goals, controlled prices, and allocated resources throughout most of the economy. During the 1950s, all of China's individual household farms were collectivized into large communes. To support rapid industrialization, the central government undertook large-scale investments in physical and human capital during the 1960s and 1970s. As a result, by 1978 nearly three-fourths of industrial production was produced by centrally controlled state-owned enterprises according to centrally planned output targets. Private enterprises and foreign-invested firms were nearly nonexistent. A central goal of the Chinese government was to make China's economy relatively self-sufficient. Foreign trade was generally limited to obtaining only those goods that could not be made or obtained in China.

Government policies kept the Chinese economy relatively stagnant and inefficient, mainly because there were few profit incentives for firms and farmers; competition was virtually nonexistent, and price and production controls caused widespread distortions in the economy. Chinese living standards were substantially lower than those of many other developing countries.

The Chinese government hoped that gradual reform would significantly increase economic growth and raise living standards.

The Introduction of Economic Reforms

Beginning in 1979, China launched several economic reforms. The central government initiated price and ownership incentives for farmers, which enabled them to sell a portion of their crops on the free market. In addition, the government established four special economic zones along the coast for the purpose of attracting foreign investment, boosting exports, and importing high technology products into China. Additional reforms, which followed in stages, sought to decentralize economic policymaking in several sectors, especially trade. Economic control of various enterprises was given to provincial and local governments, which were generally allowed to operate and compete on free market principles, rather than under the direction and guidance of state planning. Additional coastal regions and cities were designated as open cities and development zones, which allowed them to experiment with free market reforms and to offer tax and trade incentives to attract foreign investment. In addition, state price controls on a wide range of products were gradually eliminated.

China's Economic Growth Since Reforms: 1979-Present

Since the introduction of economic reforms, China's economy has grown substantially faster than during the pre-reform period (see **Table 1**). From 1960 to 1978, real annual GDP growth was estimated at 5.3% (a figure many analysts claim is overestimated, based on several economic disasters that befell the country during this time, such as the Great Leap Forward from 1958-1960 and the Cultural Revolution from 1966-1976). During the reform period (1979-the present), China's average annual real GDP grew by 9.9%; it grew by 13.0% in 2007, but slowed to 9.0% in 2008. Since 1980, economic reforms helped to produce a 14-fold increase in the size of the economy in real terms and a 11-fold increase in real per capita GDP (a common measurement of living standards).[1]

Causes of China's Economic Growth

Economists generally attribute much of China's rapid economic growth to two main factors: large-scale capital investment (financed by large domestic savings and foreign investment) and rapid productivity growth. These two factors appear to have gone together hand in hand. Economic reforms led to higher efficiency in the economy, which boosted output and increased resources for additional investment in the economy.

Table 1. China's Average Annual Real GDP Growth: 1960-2008.

Time Period	Average Annual Growth (%)
1960-1978 (pre-reform)	5.3
1979-2008 (post-reform)	9.9
1990	3.8
1991	9.3
1992	14.2
1993	14.0
1994	13.1
1995	10.9
1996	10.0
1997	9.3
1998	7.8
1999	7.6
2000	8.4
2001	8.3
2002	9.1
2003	10.0
2004	10.1
2005	9.9
2006	11.1
2007	13.0
2008	9.0

Source: Official Chinese government data and Economist Intelligence Unit.

China has historically maintained a high rate of savings. When reforms were initiated in 1979, domestic savings as a percentage of GDP stood at 32%. However, most Chinese savings during this period were generated by the profits of state-owned enterprises (SOEs), which were used by the central government for domestic investment. Economic reforms, which included the decentralization of economic production, led to substantial growth in Chinese household savings (these now account for half of Chinese domestic savings). As a result, China's gross savings as a percentage of GDP has steadily risen, reaching 52% in 2008 (compared to a U.S. rate of 8%), among the world's highest savings rates.[2]

Table 2. Comparisons of U.S., Japanese, and Chinese GDP and Per Capita GDP in Nominal U.S. Dollars and PPP, 2008

Country	Nominal GDP ($ billions)	GDP in PPP ($ billions)	Nominal Per Capita GDP	Per Capita GDP in PPP
United States	14,142	14,142	46,540	45,540
Japan	4,977	4,404	38,100	34,590
China	6	2	0	0

Source: Economist Intelligence Unit (estimated, based on World Bank Data).

Several economists have concluded that productivity gains (i.e., increases in efficiency in which inputs are used) were another major factor in China's rapid economic growth. The improvements to productivity were caused largely by a reallocation of resources to more productive uses, especially in sectors that were formerly heavily controlled by the central government, such as agriculture, trade, and services. For example, agricultural reforms boosted production, freeing workers to pursue employment in the more productive manufacturing sector. China's decentralization of the economy led to the rise of non-state enterprises, which tended to pursue more productive activities than the centrally controlled SOEs. Additionally, a greater share of the economy (mainly the export sector) was exposed to competitive forces. Local and provincial governments were allowed to establish and operate various enterprises on market principles, without interference from the central government. In addition, foreign direct investment (FDI) in China brought with it new technology and processes that boosted efficiency.

MEASURING THE SIZE OF CHINA'S ECONOMY

The actual size of China's economy has been a subject of extensive debate among economists. Measured in U.S. dollars using nominal exchange rates, China's GDP in 2008 was $4.2 trillion; its per capita GDP (a commonly used living-standards measurement) was $3,190. Such data would indicate that China's economy and living standards are significantly lower than those of the United States and Japan, respectively considered to be the number-one and number-two largest economies (see **Table 2** above).

Many economists, however, contend that using nominal exchange rates to convert Chinese data into U.S. dollars substantially underestimates the size of

China's economy. This is because prices in China for many goods and services are significantly lower than those in the United States and other developed countries. Economists have attempted to factor in these price differentials by using a purchasing power parity (PPP) measurement, which attempts to convert foreign currencies into U.S. dollars on the basis of the actual purchasing power of such currency (based on surveys of the prices of various goods and services) in each respective country. This PPP exchange rate is then used to convert foreign economic data in national currencies into U.S. dollars.

Because prices for many goods and services are significantly lower in China than in the United States and other developed countries, the PPP exchange rate nearly doubles the size of the Chinese economy from $4.2 trillion (nominal dollars) to $8.3 trillion (PPP dollars), significantly larger than Japan's GDP in PPPs ($4.4 trillion), and 58% the size of the U.S. economy. PPP data also raise China's per capita GDP from $3,190 (nominal) to $6,210.[3] The PPP figures indicate that, while the size of China's economy is substantial, its living standards (those rising) remain far below those of the U.S. and Japan. China's per capita GDP on a PPP basis was only 13.6% of U.S. levels. Thus, even if China's GDP were to overtake that of the United States in the next few decades, its living standards would likely remain substantially below those of the United States for many years to come.[4]

Foreign Direct Investment in China

China's trade and investment reforms and incentives led to a surge in foreign direct investment (FDI), which has been a major source of China's capital growth. According to Chinese data, annual utilized FDI in China grew from $636 million in 1983 to $92 billion in 2008. The cumulative level of FDI in China at the end of 2008 stood at an estimated $853 billion, making China one of the world's largest destinations of FDI.[5]

Based on cumulative FDI for 1979-2008, about 41% of FDI in China has come from Hong Kong, 10.5% from the British Virgin Islands,[6] 8.1% from Japan, and 7.5% from the United States (see **Table 3**).[7] Hong Kong was the largest investor in China in 2008, while the United States ranked sixth, accounting for 3.2% of total. Annual U.S. FDI flows to China peaked at $5.4 billion in 2002, declined annually through 2007, before increasing by 12.5% (to $2.9 billion) in 2008 (see **Figure 1**). The U.S. share of total annual FDI flows to China fell from 10.2% in 2002 to 3.2% in 2008.[8]

Table 3. Major Foreign Investors in China: 1979-2008 ($ billions and % of total)

Country	Estimated Cumulative Utilized FDI: 1979-2008		Utilized FDI in 2008		
	Amount	% of Total	Amount	% of Total	% Change over 2007
Total	852.6	100.0	92.4	100.0	23.6
Hong Kong	341.0	40.0	41.0	44.4	48.1
British Virgin Islands	89.8	10.5	16.0	17.3	-3.6
Japan	69.3	8.1	3.7	4.0	1.8
United States	64.0	7.5	2.9	3.2	12.5
Taiwan	47.6	5.6	1.9	2.1	–0.3
Singapore	37.5	4.4	4.4	4.8	39.3
South Korea	31.8	3.7	3.1	3.4	–14.8

Source: Chinese Ministry of Commerce.

Note: Ranked by cumulative top seven investors through 2008. Cumulative data by country estimated by CRS using previous years data.

The Chinese government estimates that in 2007, there were 286,200 foreign-invested companies in China. These firms employed more than 42 million people and accounted for 31.5% of gross industrial output value.[9]

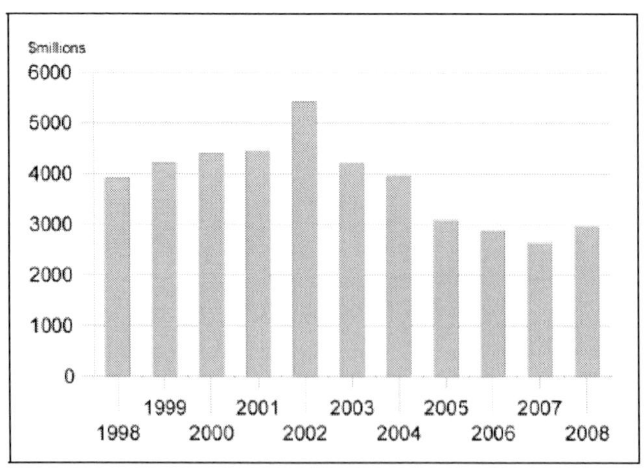

Source: Chinese Ministry of Commerce and Chinese Yearbook, various years. (Note, Chinese and U.S. data on bilateral FDI flows differ sharply).

Figure 1. U.S. FDI in China: 1998-2008.

CHINA'S TRADE PATTERNS

Economic reforms have transformed China into a major trading power. Chinese exports rose from $14 billion in 1979 to $1,429 billion in 2008, while imports over this period grew from $16 billion to $1,132 billion (see **Table 4**). In 2004, China surpassed Japan as the world's third-largest merchandise trading economy, after the European Union (EU) and the United States, and in 2007 it became the second largest exporter, surpassing the United States (and was the second largest in 2008). China's exports have grown dramatically in recent years, more than doubling in size from 2003 to 2008, with an average annual growth rate of nearly 27%. Imports over this period increased by an average of 19% per year. China's trade surplus, which totaled $32 billion in 2004, surged to $297 billion in 2008.

Merchandise trade surpluses, large-scale foreign investment, and large purchases of foreign currencies to maintain its exchange rate with the dollar and other currencies have enabled China to accumulate the world's largest foreign exchange reserves at $1.95 trillion at the end December 2008, making it the world's largest holder.

Table 4. China's Merchandise World Trade: 1979-2008 ($ billions)

Year	Exports	Imports	Trade Balance
1979	13.7	15.7	–2.0
1980	18.1	19.5	–1.4
1985	27.3	42.5	–15.3
1990	62.9	53.9	9.0
1995	148.8	132.1	16.7
2000	249.2	225.1	24.1
2001	266.2	243.6	22.6
2002	325.6	295.2	30.4
2003	438.4	412.8	25.6
2004	593.4	561.4	32.0
2005	762.0	660.1	101.9
2006	969.1	791.5	177.6
2007	1,218.0	955.8	262.2
2008	1,428.9	1,131.5	297.4

Source: *International Monetary Fund, Direction of Trade Statistics and Global Trade Atlas* (using official Chinese statistics).

China's Major Trading Partners

China's trade data often differ significantly from those of its major trading partners, including the United States. This is largely due to the large share of China's trade (both exports and imports) that pass through Hong Kong (which reverted back to Chinese rule in July 1997 but is treated as a separate customs area by most countries, including China and the United States). China treats a large share of its exports through Hong Kong as Chinese exports to Hong Kong for statistical purposes, while many countries that import Chinese products through Hong Kong generally attribute their origin to China for statistical purposes.

According to Chinese trade data, its top five trading partners in 2008 were the EU, the United States, Japan, the 10 nations that constitute the Association of Southeast Asian Nations (ASEAN), and Hong Kong. China's largest export markets in 2008 were the EU, the United States, and Japan, while its top sources for imports were Japan, the EU, and ASEAN (the United States ranked sixth). China maintained substantial trade surpluses with the United States, the EU, and Hong Kong, but reported deficits with Japan and ASEAN. China reported that it had a $171 billion trade surplus with the United States, but U.S. data show that it had a $266 billion deficit with China. These trade imbalance data disparities occur with many of China's other major trading partners as well (see **Table 5**).

Chinese data indicated that 18% of its exports went to the United States in 2008. However, many analysts contend that the United States is a much more significant market for China than its trade data indicate, and they attempt to show this by taking U.S. data on its imports from China ($338 billion in 2008) and dividing it by China's official data on its total exports ($1,429 billion), which yields about 24% (i.e., the percent of Chinese exports that go to the United States).[10]

A growing level of Chinese exports is from foreign-funded enterprises (FFEs) in China. According to Chinese data, FFEs were responsible for 55% of Chinese exports in 2008 compared with 41% in 1996. A large share of these FFEs are owned by Hong Kong and Taiwan investors, many of whom have shifted their labor-intensive, export-oriented, firms to China to take advantage of low-cost labor. A large share of the products made by such firms is likely exported to the United States.

Additional information on China's trade with other countries and regions, including Africa, Iran, and North Korea, can be found in the **Appendix**.

Table 5. China's Major Trading Partners: 2008 ($ billions)

Country	Total Trade	Chinese Exports	Chinese Imports	China's Trade Balance	Trading Partner's Reported Trade Balance With China
European Union	425.9	293.0	132.9	160.1	-247.6
United States	333.8	252.3	81.5	170.8	-266.2
Japan	266.8	116.2	150.6	–34.5	-18.6
ASEAN[a]	231.0	114.1	116.9	–2.8	n.a.
Hong Kong	203.7	190.8	12.9	177.8	-3.1
Total Chinese Trade	2,560.4	1,428.9	1,131.5	297.4	n.a.

Source: **Global Trade Atlas and World Trade Atlas using official Chinese data.**

Note: Chinese data on its bilateral trade often differ substantially from the official trade data of many of its trading partners.

a. Association of Southeast Asian Nations (ASEAN) member countries are Indonesia, Malaysia, the Philippines, Singapore, Thailand, Brunei, Cambodia, Laos, Myanmar (Burma), and Vietnam.

Major Chinese Trade Commodities

China's abundance of cheap labor (the average labor cost per hour in China was $1.35, compared with $24.50 in the United States in 2006)[11] has made it internationally competitive in many low- cost, labor-intensive manufactures. As a result, manufactured products constitute an increasingly larger share of China's trade. A substantial amount of China's imports is comprised of parts and components that are assembled in Chinese factories (major products include consumer electronic products and computers), then exported. China's top 10 exports and imports in 2008 are listed in **Table 5** and **Table 6**, respectively, using the harmonized tariff system (HTS) on a two-digit level.

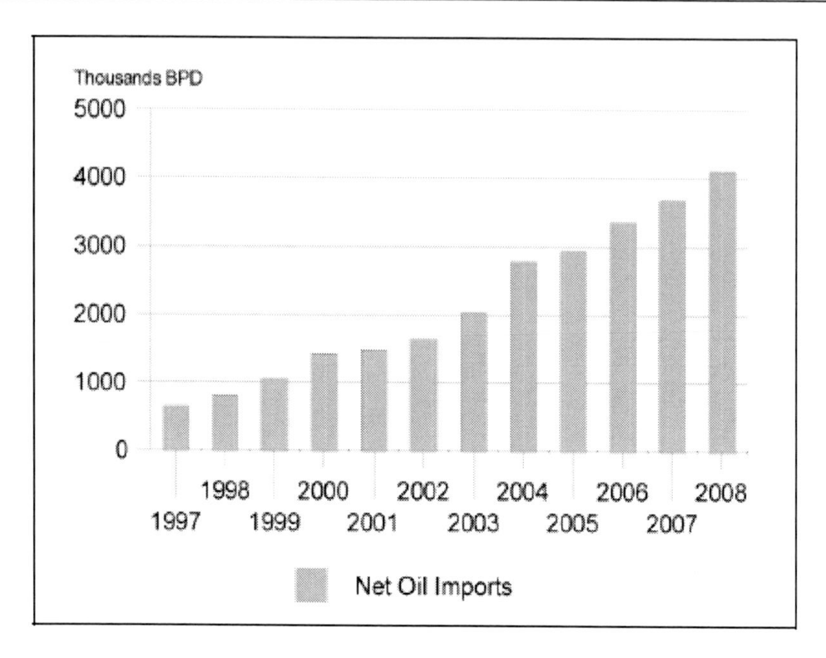

Figure 2. China's Net Oil Imports: 1997-2008.

China's Growing Appetite for Imported Oil

China's rapid economic growth has fueled a growing demand for energy, such as petroleum, and that demand is becoming an increasingly important factor in determining world oil prices. China is the world's second largest consumer of oil products (after the United States) at 7.6 million barrels per day (bpd) in 2007 (compared to 3.9 million in 1997), and that level is projected to increase to 13.6 million bpd by 2030 (depending on China's future growth and energy policies).[12] China became a net oil importer (i.e., imports minus exports) in 1993. Net oil imports grew from 632 thousand bpd in 1997 to about 4.1 million bpd in 2008. China's net oil imports doubled from 2003 to 2008 (see **Figure 2**), and making it the world's third largest net oil importer (after the United States and Japan). China's net oil imports are projected to rise to 13.1 million bpd by 2030, a level that would be comparable to the EU in that year. China's dependence on imported oil could rise from about the current level of about 50% to 80% by 2030.[13]

Table 6. Major Chinese Exports: 2008

HS	Description	$millions	Percent of Total	2008/2007 % Change
	World	1,428,869	100.0	17.3
85	Electrical machinery	342,082	23.9	13.9
84	Machinery	268,740	18.8	17.5
61	Knit apparel	60,590	4.2	-1.2
72	Iron and steel	53,494	3.7	33.9
62	Woven apparel	52,430	3.7	10.8
73	Iron and steel products	48,344	3.4	31.7
90	Optical, photographic, cinematographic, measuring checking, precision, medical or surgical instruments and apparatus; parts and accessories thereof	43,385	3.0	17.2
94	furniture and bedding	42,786	3.0	19.0
87	vehicles, not railway (mainly auto parts ,motorcycles trucks, and bicycles)	39,316	2.8	23.4
95	ment	95	2.3	20.8

Source: World Trade Atlas, using official Chinese statistics.
Notes: Top 10 exports, 2-digit level, harmonized tariff system.

CHINA'S GROWING OVERSEAS DIRECT INVESTMENT

A key aspect of China's economic growth strategy has been to attract foreign investment into China. However, in 2000, China's leaders initiated a new "go global" strategy, which sought to encourage firms (especially state-owned enterprises) to invest overseas. The Chinese government generally refers to these activities as overseas direct investment (ODI). There appears to be several factors driving this investment:

- China's massive accumulation of foreign exchange reserves has led government officials to seek more profitable ways of investing these holdings (which traditionally have mainly been put into relatively safe, low yield assets, such as U.S. Treasury securities). On September 29, 2007, the Chinese government officially launched the

China Investment Corporation (under the direction of the State Council) in an effort to better manage its foreign exchange reserves. It reportedly will initially manage over $200 billion, making it one of the world's largest sovereign wealth funds. Some analysts believe that China will increasingly use its reserves to purchase foreign firms, or shares of foreign firms, that are perceived to be profitable.

- As a developing country, China has traditionally sought to attract FDI into the country in order to, through joint ventures, gain access to foreign technology and management skills to help domestic firms become more efficient and internationally competitive. Now the Chinese government is attempting to promote the development of internationally recognized Chinese brands. One strategy has been to purchase (or attempt to purchase) existing companies and their internationally-recognized brand names (as well as to obtain technology and management skills). For example, in April 2005 Lenovo Group Limited, a Chinese computer company, purchased IBM Corporation's personal computer division for $1.75 billion.[14] On June 20, 2005, Haier Group, a major Chinese home appliances manufacturer, made a $1.28 billion bid to take over Maytag Corporation, although the bid was later withdrawn.
- Acquisition of energy and raw materials has been a major priority of China's overseas investment strategy. As such, China has sought to either purchase or invest in foreign energy and raw material companies, infrastructure projects (such as oil and gas pipelines, oil refineries, and mines), and joint ventures.[15] For example, in June 2005, the China National Offshore Oil Corporation (CNOOC), through its Hong Kong subsidiary (CNOOC Ltd.), made a bid to buy a U.S. energy company, UNOCAL, for $18.5 billion, although CNOOC later withdrew its bid due to opposition by several congressional Members. In August 2005, the China National Petroleum Corporation (CNPC), China's largest oil company, purchased PetroKazakhstan Inc., a Canadian-registered company, for $4.2 billion.[16] According to the Eurasia Group, since the 1990s CNPC has signed energy deals with Sudan worth $10 billion, with $4 billion in actual investment.[17] On February 12, 2009, a Chinese state-owned firm, Aluminum Corporation of China (Chinalco), announced it would invest $19.5 billion in Rio Tinto Group (a leading international mining group) and reportedly is the largest Chinese overseas investment to date.

Table 7. Major Chinese Imports: 2008

HS	Description	$millions	percent of total	2008/2007 % change
	World	1,131,469	100	18.3
85	Electrical machinery	266,639	23.6	3.5
27	Mineral fuel, oil etc	168,643	14.9	61.1
84	Machinery	138,707	12.3	11.5
26	Ores, slag, and ash	85,236	7.5	58.1
90	Optical, photographic, cinematographic, measuring, checking, precision, medical or surgical instruments and apparatus; parts and accessories thereof	77,696	6.9	12.0
39	Plastic	48,841	4.3	7.8
29	Organic chemicals	39,301	3.5	2.4
87	Vehicles, not railway (mainly autos and parts)	26,941	2.4	21.8
74	Copper and articles thereof	26,085	2.3	-4.0
72	Iron And Steel	20	2.2	6.6

Source: World Trade Atlas, using official Chinese statistics.
Notes: Top 10 imports in 2008, two-digit level, harmonized tariff schedule.

China is a relatively small, but quickly growing, global investor. China's annual ODI increased from $2.9 billion in 2003 to $52.2 billion in 2008; its ODI in 2008, was nearly double 2007 levels ($26.5 billion). China's cumulative ODI through 2008 was $170.1 billion.

Table 8 lists the top 10 destinations for China's cumulative ODI as of 2007. Hong Kong was by far the major destination (accounting for 58% of total), followed by the Cayman Island (14%), the British Virgin Islands (6%), and the United States (2%).[18] China's cumulative FDI in Africa through 2007 was $4.4 billion; major destinations of that ODI were South Africa, Nigeria, and the Sudan.

Some analysts contend that much of the ODI going to Hong Kong and Caribbean islands represents "round-tipping," that is, investment that is sent overseas but then re-invested elsewhere (especially) to take advantage of favorable treatment afforded to foreign investment. Some of that capital could be also going into tax havens. The largest sectors of China's cumulative ODI through 2007 included leasing and business services (26% of total), wholesale and retail trade (17%), financial intermediation (14%), and mining (13%).

Table 8. Top 10 Destinations for China's Overseas Direct Investment: 2007 ($ millions)

Country	FDI in 2007	Cumulative FDI Through 20
Hong Kong	13,732	68,781
Cayman Islands	2,602	16,811
British Virgin Islands	1,876	6,627
United States	196	1,881
Australia	532	1,444
Singapore	398	1,444
Russian Federation	478	1,422
Canada	1,033	1,255
South Korea	57	1,214
United Kingdom	567	950
Total Chinese ODI	26,505	117,911

MAJOR LONG-TERM CHALLENGES FACING THE CHINESE ECONOMY

China's economy has shown remarkable economic growth over the past several years, and many economists project that it will enjoy fairly healthy growth in the near future. However, economists caution that these projections are likely to occur only if China continues to make major reforms to its economy. Failure to implement such reforms could endanger future growth.

- **The global financial crisis**. This crisis currently poses the biggest overall threat to China's economic growth. China is highly dependent on foreign trade and investment for its economic growth and thus an economic slowdown among China's major trading partners could have a big impact on China's future growth (discussed in more detail below).

- **An inflexible currency policy**. China does not allow its currency to float and therefore must make large-scale purchases of dollars to keep the exchange rate within certain target levels. Although the yuan has appreciated someone since reforms were introduced in July 2005, analysts contend that it remains highly undervalued against the dollar.

Economists warn that China's currency policy has made the economy overly dependent on exports and fixed investment for growth and has promoted easy credit policies by the banks. These policies may undermine long-term economic stability by causing overproduction in various sectors, increasing the level of non-performing loans held by the banks and boosting inflationary pressures.[19]

- **State-owned enterprises (SOEs)**, which account for about one-third of Chinese industrial production, put a heavy strain on China's economy. By some estimates, over half lose money and must be supported by subsidies, mainly through state banks. Government support of unprofitable SOEs diverts resources away from potentially more efficient and profitable enterprises. In addition, the poor financial condition of many SOEs makes it difficult for the government to reduce trade barriers out of fear that doing so would lead to widespread bankruptcies among many SOEs and unemployment.

- **The banking system** faces several major difficulties due to its financial support of SOEs and its failure to operate solely on market-based principles. China's banking system is regulated and controlled by the central government, which sets interest rates and attempts to allocate credit to certain Chinese firms. The central government has used the banking system to keep afloat money-losing SOEs by pressuring state banks to provide low-interest loans, without which a large number of the SOEs would likely go bankrupt. According to some estimates, over 50% of state-owned bank loans go to the SOEs, even though a large share of loans are not likely to be repaid. The precarious financial state of the Chinese banking system has made Chinese reformers reluctant to open the banking sector to foreign competition. Corruption poses another problem for China's banking system because loans are often made on the basis of political connections. This system promotes widespread inefficiency in the economy because savings are generally not allocated on the basis of obtaining the highest possible returns. Many private companies in China find it difficult to borrow from state banks.

- **Growing public unrest.** The Chinese government acknowledged that there were over 87,000 protests (many of which were violent) in 2005 (compared with 53,000 protests in 2003) over such issues as pollution, government corruption, and land seizures.[20] A number of protests in China have stemmed in part from frustrations among many Chinese (especially peasants) that they are not benefitting from China's economic reforms and rapid growth, and perceptions that those who are getting rich are doing so because they have connections with government officials. Protests have broken out over government land seizures and plant shutdowns in large part due to perceptions that these actions benefitted a select group with connections. A 2005 United Nations report stated that the income gap between the urban and rural areas was among the highest in the world and warned that this gap threatens social stability. The report urged China to take greater steps to improve conditions for the rural poor, and bolster education, health care, and the social security system.[21] The global financial crisis, which has already caused significant job losses in China could lead to sharply increased levels of worker unrest.

- **The lack of the rule of law** in China has led to widespread government corruption, financial speculation, and misallocation of investment funds. In many cases, government "connections," not market forces, are the main determinant of successful firms in China. Many U.S. firms find it difficult to do business in China because rules and regulations are generally not consistent or transparent, contracts are not easily enforced, and intellectual property rights are not protected (due to the lack of an independent judicial system). The lack of the rule of law in China limits competition and undermines the efficient allocation of goods and services in the economy. Reports of slave labor in northern China in 2007, which included kidnapped children and mentally handicapped people, raised public anger over the lack of enforcement of labor laws.

- **Poor government regulatory environment**. China maintains a weak and relatively decentralized government structure to regulate economic activity in China. Laws and regulations often go unenforced or are ignored by local government officials. As a result, many firms cut corners in order to maximize profits. This has lead to a proliferation of unsafe food and consumer products being sold in China or exported abroad.[22] Lack of government enforcement of food safety laws led to a massive recall of melamine-tainted infant milk formula that reportedly killed at least four children and sickened 53,000 others in 2008. Growing concerns over the health and safety of Chinese products (such as fish, pet food, tires, and toys) in the United States and other countries could lead consumers to reduce their purchases of Chinese products and could undermine China's efforts to develop and promote internationally recognized Chinese brands.

- **Growing pollution.** The level of pollution in China continues to worsen, posing series health risks to the population. The Chinese government often disregards its own environmental laws in order to promote rapid economic growth. According to the World Bank, 20 out of 30 of the world's most polluted cities are in China, with significant costs to the economy (such as health problems, crop failures and water shortages). According to one government estimate, environmental damage costs the country $226 billion, or 10% of the country's GDP, each year. The Chinese government estimates that there are over 300 million people living in rural areas that drink unsafe water (caused by chemicals and other contaminants). Toxic spills in 2005 and 2006 threatened the water supply of millions of people. China is the largest producer and consumer of coal, which accounts for about 70% of China's energy use. Although growing environmental degradation has been recognized as a serious problem by China's central government, it has found it difficult to induce local governments to comply with environmental laws, especially when such officials feel doing so will come at the expense of economic growth.

In October 2006, the Chinese government formally outlined its goal of building a "harmonious socialist society" by taking steps (by 2020) to lessen income inequality, improve the rule of law, beef up environmental protection, reduce corruption, and improve the country's social safety net (such as expanding health care and pension coverage to rural areas). In March 2007, the Chinese National People's Congress (NPC) passed a law to strengthen property laws to help prevent local governments from unfairly seizing land from farmers, and in June 2007 it passed a new labor contract law to enhance labor rights. In addition, the government has scrambled to improve health and safety laws and regulations.

FALLOUT FROM THE CURRENT GLOBAL FINANCIAL CRISIS[23]

China's economy has suffered a sharp slow-down as a result of the global financial crisis, largely caused by a decline in foreign demand for Chinese imports. After experiencing double-digit growth in monthly exports (on a year-on-year basis) from January to October 2008 (with the exception of February), Chinese monthly exports have declined. They fell by 2.2% in November 2008, 2.8% in December 2008, and 17.5% in January 2009 (year-on year basis). During the same period, China's imports dropped even more sharply: 18.0%, 21.3%, and 43.1%, respectively. China's FDI flows have declined as well; in January they fell by 5.7% on a year-on-year basis. A

In January 2009, the Chinese government stated that 20 million migrant workers had lost their jobs due to the global financial crisis. The real estate market in several Chinese cities has exhibited signs of a bursting bubble, including a slow down in construction, falling prices, and growing levels of unoccupied buildings. In addition, the value of China's largest stock market, the Shanghai Stock Exchange Composite Index, has fallen by over 58% from January 2008 to February 2009). The Chinese government contends that its economic stimulus policies will enable the economy to grow by 8.0% in 2009. However, several economic forecasting firms doubt this can be achieved. Global Insight predicts China's real GDP growth will by 5.9%.[24]

China has taken a number of steps to stimulate its economy. On November 9, 2008, it announce that it would implement a two-year $586 billion stimulus package, mainly dedicated to infrastructure projects. Interest rates were cut twice in October and real estate taxes were cut. The government also pledged to cut export targets and boost subsidies to small and medium-sized firms.

Analysts debate what role China might play in responding to the global financial crisis, given its huge foreign exchange reserves but its relative reluctance to become a major player in global economic affairs and its tendency to be cautious with its reserves. Some have speculated that China, in order to help stabilize its most important trading partner, the United States, would boost purchases of U.S. securities (especially Treasury securities).[25] This would help the U.S. government fund the purchases of troubled assets and programs to stimulate the economy.[26] Additionally, China might try to shore up the U.S. economy by buying U.S. stocks.

On September 21, 2008, the White House indicated that President Bush had called Chinese President Hu Jintao about the financial crisis and steps the Administration was planning to take. An unnamed Chinese trade official was reported by *Inside U.S. Trade* as stating that "the purpose of that call was to ask for China's help to deal with this financial crisis by urging China to hold even more U.S. Treasury bonds and U.S. assets." The official was further quoted as saying that China recognized that it "has a stake" in the health of the U.S. economy, both as a major market for Chinese exports and in terms of preserving the value of U.S.-based assets held by China and that a stabilized U.S. economy was in China's own interest.[27] At a press conference during her visit to China on February 21, 2009, Secretary of State Hillary Rodham Clinton stated that she appreciated "greatly the Chinese government's continuing confidence in the United States treasuries." Some contend that taking an active role to help the United States (and other troubled) economies would boost China's image as a positive contributor to the world economic order, similar to what occurred during the 1997-1998 Asian financial crisis when it offered financial assistance to Thailand and pledged not to devalue its currency even though other East Asian economies had done so, a move that was highly praised by U.S. officials at the time.

On the other hand, there are a number of reasons why China would be reluctant to significantly increase its purchases of U.S. assets. One concern would be whether increased Chinese investments in the U.S. economy would produce long-term economic benefits for China. Some Chinese investments in U.S. financial companies have fared poorly, and Chinese officials would be reluctant to put additional money into investments that were deemed to be too risky.[28] Secondly, a sharp economic downturn of the Chinese economy would likely increase pressure on the government to invest money at home, rather than overseas. Many analysts (including some in China) have questioned the wisdom of China's policy of investing a large volume of foreign exchange reserves in U.S. government securities (which offer a relatively low rate of return) when China has such huge development needs at home. Many Chinese officials contend that maintaining strong economic growth in China is the most effective action China can take to promote global growth. Several economists in the West have suggested for years that China should boost domestic spending and appreciate its currency to promote more balanced growth, greater economic efficiency, and improve the country's living standards.

APPENDIX. CHINA'S GROWING ECONOMIC TIES WITH AFRICA, NORTH KOREA, AND IRAN

China has sought to expand its trade with countries around the world, especially those that posses energy and raw materials China needs to sustain its rapid economic growth, such as those in Africa. Although China's trade with these countries is relatively small (compared with its major trading partners), it is growing rapidly. China is also a major trading partner of various countries that pose challenges to U.S. foreign policy, such as Iran, Sudan, and North Korea.[29]

China-Africa Trade

China's imports from africa

China's imports from Africa as a percent of its total imports grew from 2.8% in 2004 to 3.8% in 2007 (to $36.3 billion).[30] As a whole, Africa was China's seventh largest source of imports in 2007. China's imports from Africa grew by 25.9% over the previous year (compared to total Chinese imports growth of 20.8%). Mineral fuels were by far China's largest import from Africa, accounting for 72% of total imports. Angola was China's largest source of imports from Africa, accounting for 35% of those imports in 2007, followed by South Africa, Sudan, the Congo, and Equatorial Guinea. China's imports from Sudan were up 112% over the previous year (see **Table A-1** and **Table A-2**). In 2006, China was Sudan's largest source of imports (18.2% of total).[31]

Table A-1. Top Five African Sources of Chinese Imports: 2004-2007 ($ millions)

2004		2005	2006	2007	2006-2007 % Change
Africa Total	15,641	21,114	28,768	36,330	25.9
Angola	4,718	6,581	10,931	12,885	17.9
South Africa	2,955	3,444	4,095	6,608	61.4
Sudan	1,706	2,615	1,941	4,114	111.9
Congo	1,569	2,278	2,785	2,828	1.6
torial Guinea	995	1,486	2,538	1,697	-33.1

Source: *World Trade Atlas*. Official Chinese statistics.

Table A-2. Top Five Chinese Imports from Africa: 2004-2007 ($ millions and %)

HS 2 Commodity Description	2004	2005	2006	2007	% of Total 2007	2006-2007 % Change
Mineral fuel, oil, etc	10,135	14,676	21,083	25,997	71.8	23.3
Ores, slag, ash	1,393	1,577	2,116	3,298	9.1	55.9
Precious stones and metals	742	967	1,196	1,358	3.8	13.5
Wood	473	524	705	915	2.5	29.8
Iron and steel	439	475	315	851	2.4	170.6

Source: *World Trade Atlas*. Official Chinese statistics.

Table A-3. Top Five African Suppliers of Mineral Fuel to China: 2007

Country	Imports ($millions)	Rank as a Supplier of Mineral Fuel to China
Angola	12,876	2
Sudan	4,086	7
Congo	2,307	12
Equatorial Guinea	1,566	18
Libya	1,528	19
Africa Total	97	—

Source: *Global Trade Atlas*.

China's mineral fuel imports from africa

Africa has become an important source of China's surging energy needs. In 2007, 72% of China's imports from Africa were mineral fuels. China's fuel imports from Africa rose from $10.1 billion in 2004 to $26.0 billion in 2007. In 2007, Africa supplied 24.8% of China's imported mineral fuels (compared with 9.1% in 1997). Angola was China's second largest overall mineral fuel supplier and its largest African supplier. Other major African suppliers (and the world rank) of mineral fuel to China were Sudan (7th), the Congo (12th), Equatorial Guinea (18th), and Libya (19th) (see **Table A-3**).

China's exports to africa

The share of Chinese exports going to Africa rose from 2.3% in 2004 to 3.1% in 2007 (to $37.3 billion).[32] If Africa were treated as a single trading partner, it would rank as China's seventh largest export market in 2007. Exports to Africa grew by 39.7% over the previous year (compared to China's total exports growth of 25.7%). Major Chinese exports to Africa in 2007 included electrical machinery, machinery (such as computers and components), vehicles (mainly motorcycles and trucks), apparel, and iron and steel products. The top five African destinations of Chinese exports in 2007 were South Africa, Egypt, Nigeria, Algeria, and Morocco (see **Table A-4** and **Table A-5**). In 2006, China was Sudan's second largest export market (31% of total).[33]

Table A-4. China's Top Five African Export Markets: 2004-2007 ($ millions)

Country	2004	2005	2006	2007	2006-2007 % Change
Africa Total	13,815	18,687	26,705	37,314	39.7
South Africa	2,952	3,826	5,769	7,429	28.8
Egypt	1,389	1,935	2,976	4,432	48.9
Nigeria	1,719	2,305	2,856	3,800	33.1
Algeria	981	1,405	1,952	2,709	48.8
Morocco	944	1,206	1,570	2,162	37.8

Source: *World Trade Atlas.* Official Chinese statistics.

Table A-5. Top Five Chinese Exports to Africa: 2004-2007 ($ millions)

HS 2 Commodity Description	2004	2005	2006	2007	% of Total 2007	2006-2007 % Change
Electrical machinery[a] and parts	1,905	2,799	4,122	5,806	15.6	40.9
Machinery, mechanical appliances, and parts	1,374	2,141	3,220	4,517	12.1	40.3
Vehicles (excluding railway)	936	1,448	2,023	3,165	8.5	56.4
Knit apparel	828	938	1,537	2,940	7.9	91.3
Iron/Steel products	654	903	5	0	5.1	56.7

Source: *World Trade Atlas.* Official Chinese statistics.

a. Includes electrical machinery and equipment and parts thereof; sound recorders and reproducers; television image and sound recorders and reproducers; and parts and accessories of such articles.

China's Trade with North Korea

China is North Korea's largest trading partner and a major supplier of foreign aid (largely in the form of food and fuel).[34] In 2007, Chinese exports to, and imports from, North Korea totaled $1.4 billion and $582 million, respectively. North Korea was China's 68th largest source of imports (0.06% of total) and its 68th largest export market (0.11% of total).[35] Chinese exports to North Korea rose by 13.0% and imports were up 24.3%, over 2006 levels. China accounted for 37.3% of North Korea's exports and 39.8% of its imports (2005 data).[36] According to Chinese data, its top five exports to North Korea (2007) were oil, machinery, electrical machinery (such as TVs), plastics, and vehicles (see **Table A-6**), while its top imports from North Korea were ores, coal, woven apparel, fish, and iron and steel (see **Table A-7**).

Table A-6. Major Chinese Exports to North Korea: 2004-2007 ($ millions and % change)

2004		2005	2006	2007	2006-2007 % Change
Total Exports	**795**	**1,085**	**1,232**	**1,392**	**13.0**
Mineral fuel, oil, etc. (mainly oil)	204	286	348	402	15.7
Machinery	40	77	83	104	25.0
Electrical machinery (such as TVs)	46	57	98	69	–29.0
Plastics	32	52	52	55	5.0
Vehicles	18	28	28	54	92.1

Source: *World Trade Atlas*.

Table A-7. Major Chinese Imports from North Korea: 2004-2007 ($ millions and % change)

2004		2005	2006	2007	2006-2007 % Change
Total Imports	**582**	**497**	**468**	**582**	**24.3**
Mineral fuel, oil, etc. (mainly coal)	53	112	102	170	55.1
Ores, slag, and ash	59	92	118	164	38.5
Woven apparel	49	58	63	60	–4.7
Iron and steel	75	72	35	45	28.2
Fish and seafood	261	92	43	30	–30.8

Source: *World Trade Atlas*.

China's Trade With Iran

According to the International Monetary Fund (IMF), China was Iran's largest second trading partner, after EU in 2006.[37]China was Iran's fourth largest export market (at $9.0 billion), and its second largest source of imports (at $4.9 billion). China has become an increasingly important trading partner for Iran in recent years. Iranian exports to China as a share of its total exports rose from 9.7% in 2002 to 12.9% in 2006, while Iranian imports from China as a share of its total imports increased from 4.7% to 10.6%.

Iran constitutes a relatively minor, though growing, trading partner for China. According to Chinese data, Iran was its 16th largest trading partner in 2007. China's exports to, and imports from, Iran totaled $7.3 billion and $13.3 billion, respectively. China's exports to Iran rose by 62.1% and imports from Iran were up by 33.7%. China's top exports to Iran in 2007 were iron and steel ($1.6 billion), machinery ($1.1 billion), vehicles and parts ($880 million). China's imports from Iran were dominated by crude oil, which totaled $11.6 billion and constituted 87.2% of total Chinese imports. Iran was China's third largest source of mineral fuels imports in 2007; these constituted 11.1% of China's total world oil of these products.[38] According to press reports, China's state-owned oil companies have signed oil and gas deals with Iran worth over $100 billion.[39]

End Notes

1 Source: Global Insight Database.

2 Source: EIU Database.

3 These figures represent country averages and do not reflect the growing level of income disparity in China, especially between rural areas and cities along the coast.

4 For a further discussion of PPP measurements and Chinese living standards, see CRS Report RS22808, *How Large is China's Economy? Does it Matter?*, by Wayne M. Morrison and Michael F. Martin.

5 China stopped publishing cumulative data by country after 2005. Data in table 3 reflect 2005 cumulative data and reported annual flows.

6 The British Virgin Islands is a large source of FDI because of its status as a tax haven.

7 Much of the FDI originating from the British Virgin Islands and Hong Kong may originate from other foreign investors. For example, Taiwanese businesses are believed to invest in China through other countries in order to circumvent government restrictions. In addition, some Chinese investors might be using these locations to shift funds overseas in order to re-invest in China to take advantage of preferential investment policies (this practice is often referred to as "round-tipping"). Thus the actual level of FDI in China may be overstated.

8 Note, U.S. data on bilateral FDI flows with China differ significantly with Chinese data.

[9] Gross industrial output value is the total volume of final industrial products produced and industrial services provided during a given period. Source: China 2008 Statistical Yearbook.
[10] Such calculations represent a very rough estimate and should be interpreted with caution.
[11] EIU *Industry Wire*, April 4, 2007.
[12] Global Insight, *Global Petroleum Outlook Forecast Tables (Long-Term)*, August 2008.
[13] International Energy Agency, *2007 World Energy Outlook*, p. 168. Estimates are based on Reference Scenario projections, which assume no new government policies and measures or technological breakthroughs.
[14] The Chinese government is believed to be the largest shareholder in the company.
[15] For a monthly listing of China's international activities relating to energy and raw materials, see China Institute at the University of Alberta at http://www.uofaweb.ualberta.ca/ china institute/index.cfm.
[16] *Asia Times*, August 24, 2005.
[17] Eurasia Group, *China's Overseas Investments in Oil and Gas Production*, October 16, 2006, p. 20.
[18] In terms of regions, Asia accounted for 71.0% of China's ODI, followed by Latin America (20.0%), Europe (2.8%), Africa (2.8%), North America (2.2%), and Oceania (1.1%).
[19] For further information on the economic consequences of China's currency policy, see CRS Report RL32165, *China's Currency: Economic Issues and Options for U.S. Trade Policy*, by Wayne M. Morrison and Marc Labonte.
[20] See CRS Report RL33416, *Social Unrest in China*, by Thomas Lum.
[21] *China's Human Development Report 2005.*
[22] See CRS Report RS22713, *Health and Safety Concerns Over U.S. Imports of Chinese Products: An Overview*, by Wayne M. Morrison.
[23] For additional information, see CRS Report RS22984, *China and the Global Financial Crisis: Implications for the United States*, by Wayne M. Morrison.
[24] Global Insight, *China*, February 17, 2009.
[25] In September 2008, China overtook Japan to become the largest foreign holder of U.S. Treasury securities. See CRS Report RL34314, *China's Holdings of U.S. Securities: Implications for the U.S. Economy*, by Wayne M. Morrison and Marc Labonte.
[26] Such a move would help keep U.S. interest rates relatively low. Likewise, if China decided not to sharply increase its purchases of U.S. securities, U.S. interest rates could go up.
[27] Inside U.S. Trade, China Trade Extra, September 24, 2008.
[28] For example in June 2007, China's sovereign wealth fund bought $3 billion worth of shares from Blackstone LP (a U.S. private equity firm) at $31 each, but the value of those shares fell to below $8 as of October 2008.
[29] For additional information on policy challenges posed by North Korea, see CRS Report RL33590, *North Korea's Nuclear Weapons Development and Diplomacy*, by Larry A. Niksch; and CRS Report RL32493, *The North Korean Economy: Leverage and Policy Analysis*, by Dick K. Nanto and Emma Chanlett-Avery. For information on policy challenges posed by Sudan, see CRS Report RL33574, *Sudan: The Crisis in Darfur and Status of the North-South Peace Agreement*, by Ted Dagne.
[30] In comparison, U.S. imports from Africa in 2006 were $92.0 billion. Note, the United States reports import trade data on a customs basis, while China reports imports on a cost, insurance, and freight (C.I.F.) basis. The C.I.F. basis differs from the customs basis in that the former includes the cost of insurance and freight and thus raises the value of imports (which the customs basis does not), by about 10%.
[31] Central Intelligence Agency, *the 2008 World Factbook.*
[32] In comparison, total U.S. exports to Africa in 2007 were $23.7 billion (2.0% of total U.S. exports in 2007).
[33] Central Intelligence Agency, *the 2008 World Factbook.*

[34] See CRS Report RL31785, *Foreign Assistance to North Korea*, by Mark E. Manyin; and CRS Report RL32493, *The North Korean Economy: Leverage and Policy Analysis*, by Dick K. Nanto and Emma Chanlett-Avery.

[35] Source: *World Trade Atlas*.

[36] Economist Intelligence Unit, *Country Report, North Korea*, February 2008, p. 5.

[37] China was the largest if EU countries are counted separately.

[38] *The Iran Daily* (July 25, 2007) contended that Iran had become China's largest source of oil imports.

[39] *Reuters News*, December 21, 2006

In: The Chinese Economy
Editors: Benjamin A. Tyler pp.85-95
ISBN: 978-1-60876-937-7

Chapter 4

CHINESE ECONOMY NEEDS REFORM

Jim Saxton

The People's Republic of China (PRC) is enjoying rapid economic growth. Real GDP grew at an annualized rate of 11.5 percent during the first half of 2007.[1] Yet the PRC faces significant challenges that it must overcome to sustain longterm economic growth. These include:

- Unbalanced growth
- Corruption
- Weak financial services sector
- Severe environmental degradation
- Stress on the international economy

President Hu Jintao and other senior Chinese leaders have struggled to address these issues in preparation for the 17th National Congress of the Communist Party of China that convened in Beijing on October 15, 2007.

DEVELOPMENT POLICY

Since 1992, the PRC has pursued export-led industrialization by:

- Opening to international trade and investment;

- Restructuring state-owned enterprises (SOEs) and transforming some SOEs into state- influenced enterprises (SIEs)[2] to reduce losses;
- Encouraging the development of export- oriented labor-intensive manufacturing of apparel, sporting goods, and toys and export-oriented labor-intensive final assembly of consumer electronics to employ surplus workers from rural areas and SOEs; and
- Intervening in foreign exchange markets to maintain foreign exchange rates that promote exports.

Under this policy, China has achieved rapid economic growth. From 1992 to 2006, real GDP has grown by an average of 10.3 percent a year.[3]

The PRC has successfully integrated into the global economy. In 2006, the PRC accounted for 12.9 percent of world exports and 8.9 percent of world imports (excluding intra-EU trade).[4]

To power growth and expand trade, China relied very heavily on inward foreign direct investment (FDI) by foreign multinational firms (MNFs) in Chinese subsidiaries. Cumulative inward FDI was $703 billion (equal to 25.4 percent of GDP) at year-end 2006.[5] Chinese subsidiaries of foreign MNFs accounted for 58.2 percent of China's exports and 59.7 percent of its imports in 2006.[6]

The PRC has very few Chinese MNFs. Until recently, outward FDI was mainly in natural resources by state-owned oil and mining firms. Unlike other populous economies, few Chinese firms have designed their own products and created internationally recognized brands. Instead, Chinese firms are mainly contract manufacturers for foreign firms.

UNBALANCED GROWTH

The Chinese economy is becoming very unbalanced:

- Growth depends heavily on international trade. In 2006, China's two-way trade in goods and services equaled 72.1 percent of GDP.[7] This is far higher than other populous economies.
- Since 2000, the PRC's central bank, the People's Bank of China (PBC), has intervened massively in foreign exchange markets to maintain the foreign exchange value of the renminbi within its target range. At year end 2006, the PBC had accumulated foreign exchange

reserves of $1 .066 trillion (equal to 40.3 percent of GDP).[8] In the first half 2007, the PBC's reserves grew by 25 percent to $1.333 trillion.

- Inflation is accelerating. In August 2007, consumer prices were up 6.6 percent from a year ago.[9] Domestic inflation is now affecting China's export sector. After five years of decline, the prices of Chinese manufactured exports are now increasing.[10] The PBC's ability to sterilize its rapidly increasing foreign exchange reserves may be reaching its limit. In September 2007, the State Council deferred its plan to increase state-controlled energy prices gradually to market levels to encourage energy efficiency and reduce pollution. Instead, the State Council resorted to the palliative of a freeze in state-controlled prices until the end of 2007.[11]
- Growth depends heavily on investment in fixed assets. In 2006, gross investment was 40.9 percent of GDP.[12] Although SOEs and SIEs employed 35.6 percent of urban workers and 30.5 percent of rural workers, SOEs and SIEs still accounted for about three-quarters of all investment in fixed assets in 2006.[13]
- Since 1992, real per capita income increased in all areas and among all classes. However, income inequality between cities and rural areas and among urban households has become acute:
  - From 1992 to 2006, average real per capita income expanded by 217 percent to 11,744 yuan among urban households but only by 120 percent to 4,640 yuan among rural households (in constant 2000 yuan).[14]
  - In cities, shortages of managerial, technical, and professional workers have increased their compensation. Consequently, the ratio of real per capita income in the lowest income urban households and real per capita income in the highest income urban households exploded from 3.25 in 1992 to 9.25 in 2005.[15]
- The failure to replace Mao's "iron rice bowl" system[16] with a comprehensive system of disability insurance, health insurance, and retirement saving plans has forced Chinese households to save an extraordinarily high share of their income. Because many small- to medium-size enterprises have found it difficult to obtain credit from Chinese banks, these firms save a large percentage of their profits to finance future investments. Because of both factors, the gross saving rate was 49.8 percent of GDP in 2006.[17]

Prior to the Congress, President Hu announced a series of policies that he named the "harmonious society" to reduce income disparities. These initiatives include abolishing a two-millennium-old agricultural tax, expanding health care facilities to 80 percent of rural areas, and increasing the availability of credit to small enterprises in rural areas.

During his speech at the Congress, Hu set a goal to double China's per capita real GDP and eliminate absolute poverty by 2020. He favored a greater reliance on domestic consumption and services and less dependence on international trade and manufacturing for China's future growth, but did not offer specific proposals to implement this rebalancing.

CORRUPTION

The "rule of law" remains weak. In March 2007, the National People's Congress enacted a law giving equal protection to state and private property after 13 years of debate. Despite this progress, individuals and private firms still rely to a large degree on *guanxi* (i.e., connections) with officials to protect themselves and their property.

While the PRC is nominally a unitary state, it has many levels of subsidiary government – provinces, prefectures, cities, counties, towns, and villages. The Chinese government is organized as a matrix. Each department in the central government is paired with similar departments in subsidiary governments. Policy is vertical (i.e., the heads of central government departments determine policy and direct its implementation through similar departments in subsidiary governments), but administration is horizontal (i.e., the heads of subsidiary governments make personnel decisions and fund the operations of all departments in their subsidiaries).

Since 1992, *de facto* political decentralization has allowed officials in subsidiary governments to exploit their *guanxi* to enrich themselves through corruption. Central government officials have encountered difficulties in implementing many policies. Employees of subsidiary governments have greater loyalty to officials in their subsidiary than to department heads in Beijing. The Chinese use an old proverb to describe this problem, "The mountain is high, and the emperor is far away."

Corruption is pervasive in China. According to Transparency International, the PRC scored 3.3, 70th of 163 countries, on its *Corruption Perceptions Index 2006* (10 is corruption-free), which measures corruption within a country, and 4.94, 29th of the 30 largest exporting countries, on its *Bribery Payers Index 2006* (10 is no bribery), which measures the propensity of domestic MNFs to bribe when operating abroad.[18]

In 2006, 825 senior officials were convicted for corruption, while more than 40,000 other officials and government employees were under investigation.[19] Outside of government, corruption is rampant in the state-influenced banking, real estate development, and construction industries.

Three manifestations of corruption have gained widespread attention in recent months:

- **Uncompensated property seizures.** Local officials have frequently seized farms and urban residences for development, from which these officials financially benefit, without paying adequate compensation to long-term lessees. Uncompensated seizures have caused frequent and sometimes violent protests. Attracting nationwide attention this spring, one family in Chongqing refused to relinquish its house until the local government agreed to compensate the family with another house elsewhere in city.

- **Pollution.** Local officials have repeatedly accepted bribes to allow Chinese firms to pollute and have threatened to remove, demote, or otherwise retaliate against government employees that would enforce environmental laws. In December 2006, the Director of the State Environmental Protection Administration Zhou Shengxian observed, "The failure to abide by the law, lax law enforcement, and allowing lawbreakers to go free are still serious problems in many places."[20]

- **Unsafe and counterfeit goods.** Local officials have frequently accepted bribes to allow Chinese firms to sell both unsafe goods and counterfeit goods. In recent months, the Chinese press has reported the sale of tainted goods, including food products and toothpaste, to Chinese consumers. This quality problem is now spreading to Chinese exports. Over the summer, Mattel recalled 19 million toys made by Chinese firms that were tainted with lead paint or contained loose magnets. Another one million toy ovens have been recalled because children may suffer burns from getting their fingers caught in the door. A reputation for unsafe goods is a potentially serious threat to the Chinese economy. At a meeting of the World Economic Forum prior to the APEC summit meeting in Sydney, Premier Wen Jiabao stated, "The Chinese government takes product quality and food safety very seriously."[21] Senior leaders understand that growing safety concerns could make consumers wary of buying goods made in China, and could induce foreign MNFs to give manufacturing contracts to firms in other countries. In July, Zheng Xiaoyu, the head of the State Food and Drug Administration from 1998 to 2005, was executed for accepting bribes to allow the sale of unsafe pharmaceuticals. The State Council recently directed Vice Premier Wu Yi to launch a "special war" on inadequate regulations to achieve 20 specific product safety goals by year-end.[22]

WEAK FINANCIAL SERVICES SECTOR

China's financial sector is bank-centric and state-influenced. At year-end 2006, loans at commercial banks and other depository institutions equaled 102 percent of China's GDP and accounted for 87 percent of China's domestic finance.[23]

Four major state-owned commercial banks (SOCBs) inherited billions of non-performing loans (NPLs) from the central planning era. To prepare the SOCBs to operate on a market-basis, the State Council transferred $170 billion of NPLs to four asset management corporations and injected $98 billion into the China Construction Bank (CCB), the Bank of China (BOC), and the Industrial Commercial Bank of China (ICBC) over the last decade.[24] The State Council has also injected $21 billion into credit unions and is planning to inject $40 billion into the Agriculture Bank (AB) later in 2007.[25]

Three of the four SOCBs have offered minority shares on the Hong Kong or Shanghai exchanges. The CCB raised $8 billion in October 2005; BOC, $9.7 billion in May 2006; and ICBC, $19.1 billion in October 2006. The largest joint-stock bank (JSB), the Bank of Communications, was listed on the Hong Kong exchange in June 2005.[26]

Foreign banks and financial institutions have become minority shareholders and strategic partners with CCB, BOC, ICBC, nine JSBs, and a number of urban banks.[27] Through these alliances, Chinese banks have improved their backroom operations.[28]

However, Chinese banks still extend most of their loans to SOEs and SIEs. At year-end 2006, 65 percent of bank loans were extended to SOEs and

SIEs; 24 percent, to private Chinese firms and Chinese subsidiaries of foreign MNFs, and 11 percent, to Chinese consumers.[29]

Chinese banks have not yet developed a strong credit culture. In 2006, the IMF found, "pricing of credit risk remains undifferentiated and banks do not appear to take enterprise profitability into account when making lending decision."[30]

The ratio of NPLs to total loans in all banks and depository institutions fell to 7.1 percent by yearend 2006.[31] However, significant non-market lending, probably as the result of corruption, is continuing. Without a strong credit culture, Chinese banks may be creating new mountains of NPLs. In a debt sustainability analysis, the IMF assumed that 16 percent of all new loans are likely to go bad.[32]

Since 2000, non-market lending to SOEs and SIEs has distorted China's industrial structure:

- Many of the remaining SOEs and SIEs are in capital-, energy-, and pollution-intensive heavy industries (including steel, non-ferrous metals, cement, glass, paper, and basic chemicals) in which China does not have a natural comparative advantage. In 2006, China produced 49 percent of world output in flat glass, 48 percent in cement, 35 percent in steel, and 28 percent in aluminum.
- Non-market lending has slowed the growth of small- to medium-size enterprises, real wages, and employment opportunities for less skilled Chinese workers by tilting investment away from labor-intensive, less polluting light industries and services in which China has a natural comparative advantage. Because of these labor market effects, non-market lending has contributed to a decline in household income as a share of GDP during the last decade.[33]
- Non-market lending has permitted too many small, provincially based, uncompetitive SOEs and SIEs to survive in the same industry. In 2006, for example, China had 6,959 steel firms. The combined domestic market share of the top three Chinese steel firms was 14.1 percent compared with 44.7 percent in the European Union, 63.9 percent in Japan, and 59.7 percent in the United States.[34]
- Despite growing domestic demand, excessive investment induced by non-market lending has created significant overcapacity. In 2005, for example, China's excess steel capacity of 120 million metric tons exceeded the 112.5 million metric tons of steel output of Japan.[35] In turn, overcapacity and favorable exchange rates have encouraged

SOEs and SIEs to export their excess production rather than to consolidate and downsize.

Severe Environmental Degradation

Environment pollution has become acute in China. The World Bank found that pollution cost China an amount equal to 5.8 percent of GDP in 2003.[36]

- The PRC is the largest emitter of sulfur dioxide and greenhouse gases in the world. Sixteen of the 20 cities with the most polluted air in the world are in China. Seventy-five percent of all urban residents breathe seriously unhealthy air.[37]
- Seventy-five percent of river water and 90 percent of groundwater near cities is unsafe for human use. Fifty percent of river water is also unsafe for agricultural or industrial use. Beijing and other cities in northern China are threatened with shortages of potable water.[38]
- Less than half of approximately 40 tons of toxic waste generated annually are treated or reused.[39]

These severe problems have prompted unrest. In April 2005, for example, 60,000 farmers in Zhejiang Province protested against pollution from thirteen chemical plants in an industrial park near Huaxi village that spoiled crops.[40]

Stress on the International Economy

China's unbalanced economic growth is straining the international economy. The PBC's foreign exchange interventions have contributed to the PRC's growing current account surpluses. Without these interventions:

- An appreciation in the foreign exchange value of the renminbi would increase the real income of the Chinese people. Higher real incomes would enable the Chinese to consume more goods and services, especially imports whose prices in yuan would fall relative to their domestic competitors as the renminbi appreciated;
- Some of China's manufacturing capacity that is now producing goods for exports would be redirected toward the domestic market; and

- Without the PBC's ongoing interventions in foreign exchange markets, the PBC would be unable to use the U.S. dollars that these interventions generate to acquire more U.S. financial assets. As a result, the United States would have lower current account deficit, while the PRC would have a lower current account surplus.

The PRC's large and growing current account surplus is fanning protectionist sentiments in the United States, the European Union, and other countries. Such sentiments could eventually result in protectionist legislation that could undermine an open trading system on which China's export-led development strategy depends.

Until recently, the PBC had invested a large percentage of its reserves in U.S. Treasury and agency debt securities. In early 2007, however, the State Council established a foreign exchange management company to diversify the investment of approximately $200 billion of reserves away from U.S. Treasuries and agencies into other assets.

Unlike a private individual or firm, a government agency may not make its investment decisions based solely on wealth maximization using risk and return criteria. Instead, a government agency may forgo wealth maximization to pursue non-economic objectives. For example, a government agency could buy a large minority stake in a publicly traded corporation and use its equity position to press management to pursue certain political objectives. In the United States during the 1980s, for example, state and local government pension funds sold or threatened to sell their shares in corporations doing business in South Africa to enforce an economic boycott to end apartheid. It is unknown what criteria this Chinese company will use to make its investment decisions.

CONCLUSION

It is easy to assume that the PRC will continue to enjoy double-digit economic growth into the indefinite future. However, China must confront and resolve a number of significant challenges to sustain long-term economic growth. The PRC's senior leaders are aware of these problems. During his speech at the 17th Party Congress on October 15, 2007, President Hu recognized the need for additional reforms to rebalance the Chinese economy and to sustain its growth over the long-term. However, Hu did not detail specific policy changes. Widespread corruption and *de facto* decentralization may limit Hu's ability to address these challenges quickly and effectively. It remains to be seen what reforms Hu will try to implement and how successful these reforms will be.

End Notes

[1] China National Bureau of Statistics (CNBS)/Haver Analytics.

[2] At the 15th Party Congress in 1997, President Jiang Zemin announced the *zhuada fangxiao* policy (i.e., grab the big, dump the small). Under this policy, the central government retained ownership of SOEs that produce defense goods and services, are in industrial sectors targeted for economic development, or are hopelessly insolvent, but employ millions. The central government transformed many of the other large SOEs into shareholding enterprises by issuing minority shares to investors. While shareholding enterprises exhibit many of the characteristics of private corporations, the central government still exercises effective control over their operations. These shareholding enterprises along with collective enterprises owned by subsidiary governments, cooperative enterprises in urban areas, township and village enterprises in rural areas, and private firms owned by senior officials, are collectively known as state- influenced enterprises (SIEs).

[3] CNBS/Haver Analytics.

[4] International Monetary Fund (IMF)/Haver Analytics. Calculations by author.

[5] CNBS/Haver Analytics.

[6] China General Administration of Customs and State Administration for Foreign Exchange/ Haver Analytics.

[7] IMF and CNBS/Haver Analytics. Calculations by author.

[8] CNBS/Haver Analytics.

[9] Ibid.

[10] Tom Mitchell and Geoff Dyer, "Heat in the Workshop: The 'China Price' is under Upward Pressure," *Financial Times* (October 15, 2007).

[11] Andrew Batson, "China Is in Bind to Raise Energy Prices: Efforts to Relax Controls Are Losing Out to the Fight Against Inflation," *Wall Street Journal* (September 21, 2007). Found at: http://online.wsj.com/article/SB119028617841133714.html?mod=hps_ asia_whats_ news.

[12] CNBS/Haver Analytics. Calculations by author.

[13] Ibid. Calculations by author.

[14] Ibid. Calculations by author.

[15] Ibid. Calculations by author.

[16] Under Mao's "iron rice bowl" system, SOEs provided their workers with comprehensive social-welfare benefits.

[17] CNBS/Haver Analytics.

[18] *Transparency International Corruptions Perceptions Index 2006*, and *Transparency International Bribery Payers Index 2006*, found at http://transparency.

[19] Found at: http://www.chinabalancesheet.org/Documents/Corruptio n.pdf.

[20] Associated Press, "Corruption Blamed in China's Pollution" (December 26, 2006).

[21] Ian Johnson, "Beijing Steps Up Battle for Quality," *Wall Street Journal* (September 7, 2007), A-6.

[22] Stratfor Global Intelligence Brief, "China: Product Quality, Reform and the Rule of Law," (August 27, 2007).

[23] At year-end 2006, four state-owned commercial banks (SOCBs) controlled $2.83 billion or 57.8 percent of all deposits; thirteen joint-stock banks (JSBs), $853 million or 17.4 percent; and credit unions, $440 million or 9.0 percent; 117 urban banks, $305 million or 6.1 percent; three state-owned policy banks, $297 million or 6.1 percent; and foreign banks, $93 million or 1.9 percent.
Recently, the China Banking Regulatory Commission authorized China Post to open a Postal Saving Bank in early 2007. This new institution is expected to garner about 5 percent of all deposits.
Both SOCBs and JSBs operate throughout China. The central government is the majority shareholder in the SOCBs, while SOEs and SIEs are the majority shareholders in most JSBs. Urban banks, in which local governments are majority shareholders, operate within a particular city.

[24] Donald J. S. Brean, "Banking Reform in China: What It Means for the World," Asia-Pacific Foundation of Canada (January 2007).

[25] "US$40 bil. Reportedly Earmarked for Agricultural Bank of China Bailout," *Global Insight* (August 6, 2007).

[26] Donald J. S. Brean, "Banking Reform in China: What It Means for the World," Asia-Pacific Foundation of Canada (January 2007).

[27] Among the major foreign investors/strategic partners are Royal Bank of Scotland, Merrill Lynch, Temasek, UBS, and the Asian Development Bank in BOC; Bank of America and Temasek in CCB; Goldman Sachs, Allianz, and American Express in ICBC; HSBC in Bank of Communications; Standard Chartered Bank in Bohai Bank; Asian Development Bank in China Everbright Bank; BBVA in Citic Bank; Deutsche Bank, Pangaea Capital, Hang Sang Bank and International Finance Corporation in Industrial Bank; International Finance Corporation and Asia Finance Holding in Minsheng Bank; Citigroup in Shanghai Pudong Development Bank; and Newbridge Capital in Shenzhen Development Bank.

[28] Syetarn Hansakul, "China's Banking Sector: Ripe for the Next Stage, *Deutsche Bank Research* (December 7, 2007).

[29] People's Bank of China/Haver Analytics. Diana Farrell, Susan Lund, Jaeson Rosenfeld, Fabrice Morin, Niyati Gupta, and Ezra Greenberg, *Putting China's Capital to Work: The Value of Financial System Reform* (McKinsey Institute, April 2006). Percentage calculations by author.

[30] Richard Podpiera, "Progress in China's Banking Sector Reform: Has Bank Behavior Changed?" IMF Working Paper WP/06/71 (March 2006).

[31] China Banking Regulatory Commission/Haver Analytics.

[32] International Monetary Fund, "People's Republic of China: 2006 Article IV Consultations," (October 2006), 40. Found at: http://www.imf.org/external/pubs/ft/scr/2006/cr06394.pdf.

[33] Nicholas Lardy, "China Rebalancing Economic Growth," (2007), 8. http://www.china balance sheet.org/Documents/01Rebala ncingEconGrowth.pdf See also, Jahangir Aziz and Li Cui, "Expanding China's Low Consumption: The Neglected Role of Household Income," IMF Working Paper WP/07/181 (July 2007).

[34] Daniel H. Rosen and Trevor Houser, "What Drives China's Demand for Energy" (2007), 39. Found at: http://www.chinabalancesheet.org/Documents/02WhatDr ivesChinasDemand.pdf.

[35] Lardy, 6.

[36] World Bank, *Cost of Pollution in China: Economic Estimates of Physical Damages* (2007).

[37] Jennifer L. Turner, "China's Environmental Crisis: Opening Up Opportunities for Internal Reform and International Cooperation," (March 2006). Found at: http://www.chinabalance sheet.org/Documents/Paper_Environment _Paper.PDF.

[38] Ibid.

[39] Ibid.

[40] Ibid.

In: The Chinese Economy
Editors: Benjamin A. Tyler pp.97-114
ISBN: 978-1-60876-937-7

Chapter 5

CHINESE FX INTERVENTIONS CAUSED INTERNATIONAL IMBALANCES, CONTRIBUTED TO U.S. HOUSING BUBBLE

Jim Saxton

EXECUTIVE SUMMARY

For a decade prior to 2005, the People's Republic of China (PRC) pegged its currency, the renminbi, to the U.S. dollar. On July 21 of that year, the PRC finally broke this peg. However, the PRC has continued to intervene heavily in foreign exchange markets to limit the subsequent appreciation of the renminbi. Governments in other Asian economies have sought to limit the appreciation of their currencies against both the renminbi and the U.S. dollar to maintain the price competitiveness of their manufactured exports with their Chinese rivals in North American and European markets. Shadowing the PRC's exchange rate policy, other Asian governments have also intervened heavily in foreign exchange markets. From 2001 to 2007, the PRC, India, Indonesia, Japan, South Korea, Malaysia, Taiwan, and Thailand have collectively added $2.7 trillion to their foreign exchange reserves. About 2/3 of these reserves have been invested in U.S. dollar-denominated assets, primarily U.S. Treasury and agency debt securities.

Since 2000, the PRC's exchange rate policy and the shadow policies of other Asian governments slowed the depreciation of the U.S. dollar and lowered interest rates, particularly at the long end of the yield curve. By distorting market price signals, these policies have exacerbated a number of economic problems not only in the United States but also around the world:

- These policies have contributed to the growth of unsustainable imbalances in the international accounts of both the PRC and the United States.
- The PRC's massive accumulation of foreign exchange reserves is stoking rapidly rising inflation in China.
- Low long-term interest rates contributed to the housing price bubble during the first half of this decade. As the bubble approached its peak, reckless lending became rampant.
- The bursting of this bubble revealed significant overinvestment and malinvestment in housing in the United States as well as significant speculative excesses in credit markets around the world.
- The inevitable unwinding of these imbalances, the liquidation of overinvestment and malinvestment in housing, and the restoration of confidence in credit markets may slow real GDP growth in the United States for several years.

I. INTRODUCTION

During the 1980s and 1990s, the foreign exchange value of the U.S. dollar was largely determined by the market-based, wealth-maximizing decisions of households and firms both here and abroad. Since 2000, however, the strategic interventions by central banks in foreign exchange markets have played a far larger role in determining the foreign exchange value of the U.S. dollar than during the two previous decades. In the last five years, the value of the U.S. dollar has declined (see Graph 1).

For a decade prior to 2005, the People's Republic of China (PRC) pegged its currency, the renminbi,[1] to the U.S. dollar. On July 21 of that year, the PRC broke this peg and finally allowed the value of its currency to rise, but not to a market-determined level. The People's Bank of China (PBC) continued to intervene heavily in foreign exchange markets to limit the subsequent appreciation of the renminbi. Governments in other developing and newly industrializing economies in northeast, southeast, and south Asia feared that significant appreciations of their currencies would cause their manufactured exports to lose their price competitiveness with their Chinese rivals in North American and European markets. Consequently, these governments have sought to limit the appreciation of their currencies against both the renminbi and the U.S. dollar.

Shadowing the PRC's exchange rate policy, the central banks in other Asian economies have also intervened heavily in foreign exchange markets since 2000. From 2001 to 2007, central banks in China, India, Indonesia, Japan, South Korea, Malaysia, Taiwan, and Thailand added $2.7 trillion to their foreign exchange reserves. About 2/3 of these reserves have been invested in U.S. dollar-denominated assets, primarily U.S. Treasury and agency debt securities.[2]

Since 2000, the PRC's exchange rate policy and the shadow policies of other Asian governments have kept dollar-denominated interest rates low, particularly at the long end of the yield curve, in the United States and to a lesser extent in Australia, Canada, and Europe. These policies also slowed the depreciation in the foreign exchange value of the U.S. dollar. Without massive interventions by the PRC and other Asian governments, long-term interest rates in the United States would have been significantly higher, and the foreign exchange value of the U.S. dollar would have been even lower.

By distorting market price signals, the PRC's exchange rate policy and the shadow policies of other Asian governments have exacerbated a number of economic problems not only in the United States but also around the world:

- These policies have contributed to the growth of unsustainable imbalances in the international accounts of both the PRC and the United States.[3]
- The PRC's massive accumulation of foreign exchange reserves is stoking rapidly rising inflation in China.
- Low long-term interest rates contributed to a housing price bubble in the United States. As the bubble approached its peak in 2006, reckless lending became rampant.
- The bursting of this bubble revealed significant overinvestment and malinvestment in housing in the United States as well as significant speculative excesses in credit markets around the world [4]
- The inevitable unwinding of these imbalances, the liquidation of overinvestment and malinvestment in housing, and the restoration of confidence in credit markets may slow real GDP growth in the United States for several years.

II. How Economic Factors Determine Exchange Rates and International Accounts

Under the Bretton Woods system (1945 to 1971), exchange rates were fixed. Current account transactions such as payments for imported goods were generally unregulated, but capital controls restricted both inward and outward investment transactions. International imbalances were resolved mainly through official flows of gold or U.S. dollars among central banks.

In 1973, the United States and other developed countries allowed market forces to determine the foreign exchange value of their currencies. Economists refer to this system as floating exchange rates. Over the next decade, developed and many developing countries abolished capital controls, freeing their residents to make outward foreign investment and opening their economies to inward foreign investment. In recent decades, international imbalances have been resolved mainly through market-determined changes in exchanges rates. Under floating exchange rates, a government may affect the foreign exchange value of its currency (1) through domestic monetary policy or (2) through its fiscal, regulatory, tax, trade, and other economic policies. Domestic monetary policy determines the supply of money. Changes in this supply relative to international demand affect the exchange rates of one currency with other currencies. Other economic policies affect the international demand for a country's currency by changing market expectations for the risk-adjusted after-tax rate of return. Since foreign residents must exchange their currencies to invest in other countries, policies that increase the expected risk-adjusted after-tax rate of return in one country will increase the foreign exchange value of its currency, and vice versa.

Exchange rates are also affected by the monetary policy decisions of foreign governments. If a foreign central bank were to increase the money supply of its currency faster than the growth in demand for its currency while the Federal Reserve kept the supply of U.S. dollars in line with the demand for U.S. dollars, then the exchange rate of the U.S. dollar is likely to appreciate against this foreign currency.

A policy-induced shift in either the supply of a country's currency or its international demand also changes such country's international accounts. An increase in inward foreign direct and portfolio investment will increase a country's capital and financial surplus (or reduce its deficit). This change automatically causes a country's current account deficit to increase (or its surplus to fall). Usually, this occurs through an increase in a country's trade deficit (or a decrease in its surplus) as the higher foreign exchange value of this country's currency simultaneously increases export prices in terms of other currencies and decreases import prices in terms of its own currency.

Between 1973 and 2000, official interventions by the U.S. Treasury and foreign central banks were limited and did not have a sustained influence on exchange rates. Portfolio investors can buy or sell financial assets almost instantaneously with minimal transaction costs to seek higher risk-adjusted after- tax returns, while trade and direct investment transactions often involve long-term contracts and commitments. Consequently, portfolio investment transactions by private households and firms rather than trade transactions or direct investment transactions have generally driven exchange rate fluctuations.

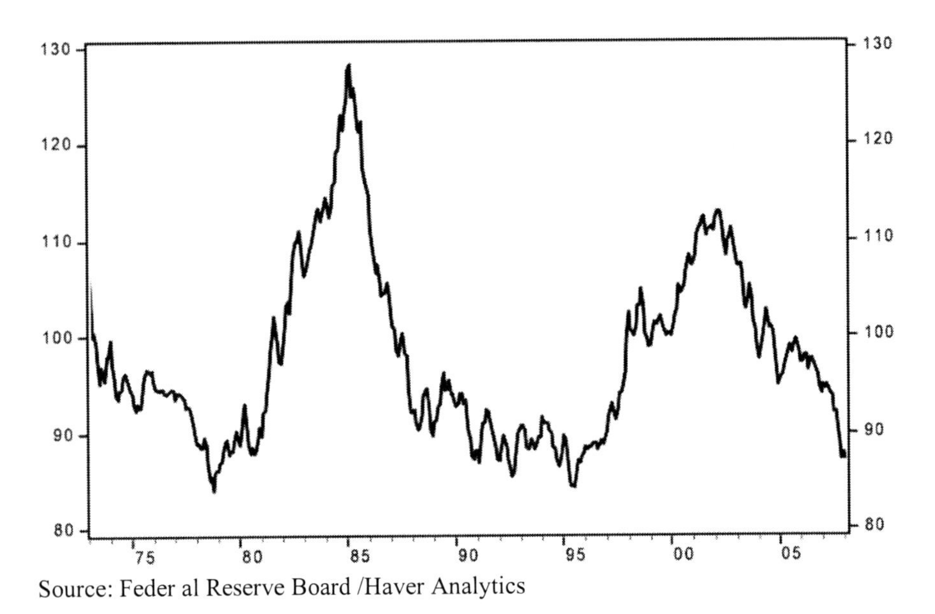

Source: Feder al Reserve Board /Haver Analytics

Graph 1. Real Broad Trade-Weighted Exchange Value of the US$ Mar -73=100

Both the disinflationary monetary policy pursued by the Federal Reserve and the Reagan administration policies of deregulation and marginal tax rate reductions increased expectations for higher risk-adjusted after-tax rates of return on U.S. investments. This drove a surge of inward private foreign investment in the early 1980s that increased the real foreign exchange value of the U.S. dollar. Again in the late 1990s, a high technology boom, trade liberalization, and a capital gains tax reduction drove another surge of inward private foreign investment, boosting the real foreign exchange value of the U.S. dollar. After these portfolio reallocations toward U.S. dollar-denominated assets peaked in 1985 and 2002, the real foreign exchange value of the U.S. dollar fell (see Graph 1).

III. MASSIVE INTERVENTION SINCE 2000

After 2000, official transactions by the People's Bank of China and central banks in other Asian economies exerted significant upward pressure on the foreign exchange value of the U.S. dollar to keep the prices of their exports competitive. The PBC pegged the renminbi to the U.S. dollar through July 20, 2005, and thereafter allowed the renminbi to appreciate very gradually against the U.S. dollar. To maintain this peg and then to keep the renminbi from appreciating more rapidly to a market-determined level, China intervened heavily in foreign exchange markets by buying dollars and selling yuan. The PRC 's foreign exchange reserves ballooned by $1 .363 trillion since December 31, 2000 to $1 .528 trillion on December 31, 2007. At year-end, the PRC's foreign exchange reserves were 34.7 percent of GDP (see Graph 2A). To contain the inflationary effects of issuing so many yuan, the PBC has tried to sterilize its foreign exchange interventions by issuing yuan-denominated bonds and increasing the reserve requirements for Chinese banks and other depository institutions. The PBC has used its dollars to purchase foreign debt securities, about two-thirds of which are believed to be U.S. dollar-denominated.

Fearing a loss of the price competitiveness of their exports, central banks in other Asian economies have intervened in foreign exchange markets to prevent a significant appreciation of their currencies against the renminbi. From December 31, 2000 to December 31, 2007, the foreign exchange reserves grew by $164 billion in Taiwan, $543 billion in India, Indonesia, South Korea, Malaysia, and Thailand combined, and $601 billion in Japan. Thus, central banks in China, India, Indonesia, Japan, South Korea, Malaysia, Taiwan, and Thailand have collectively added $2,671 billion to their foreign exchange reserves.

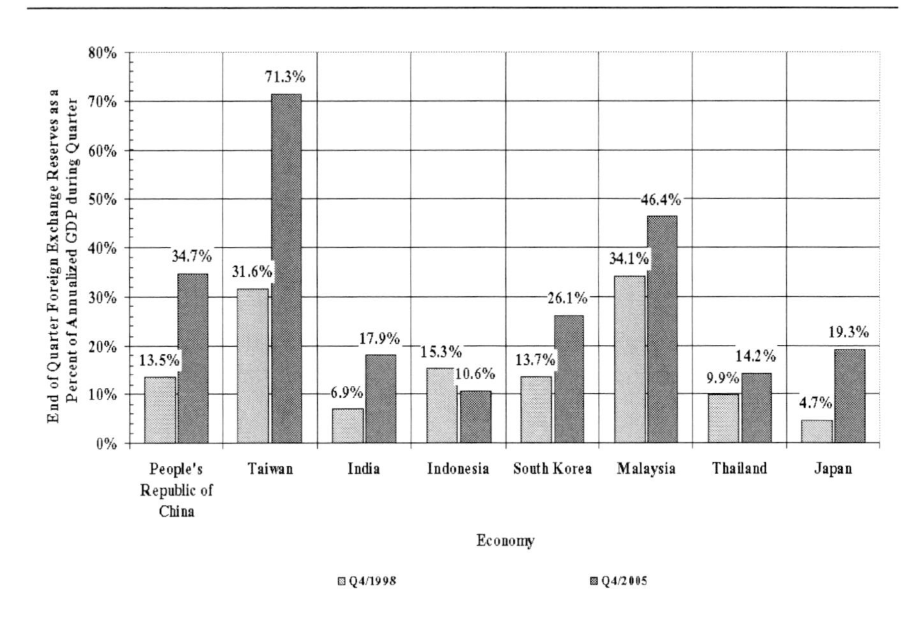

Graph 2A. Accumulation of Large Foreign Exchange Reserves in Asia

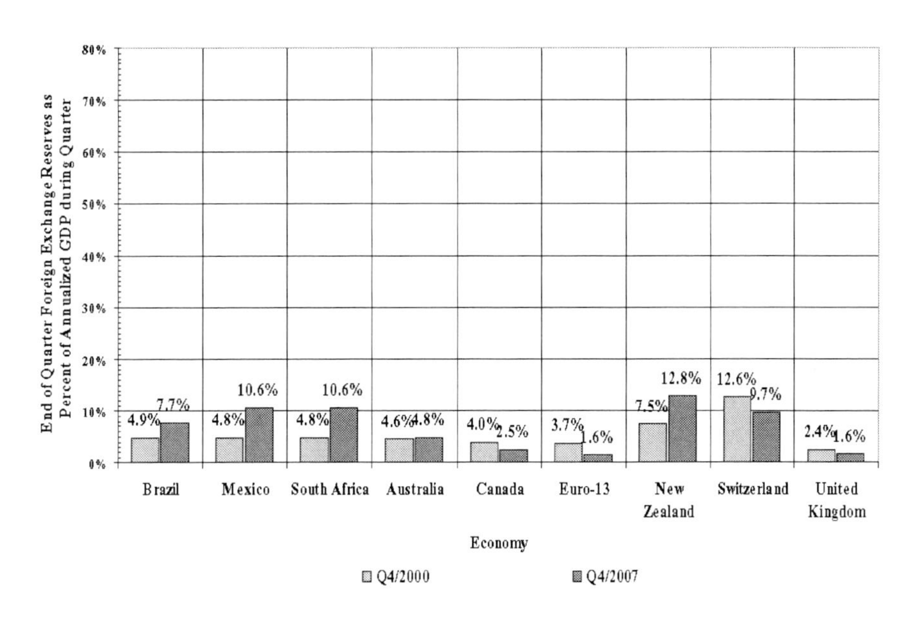

Graph 2B. Moderate Changes in Foreign Exchange Reserves in Major Developed and Developing Economies Outside of Asia

Graph 2A also shows how other Asian economies accumulated large foreign exchange reserves relative to their GDP from year-end 2000 to year-end 2007. On December 31, 2007, foreign exchange reserves totaled $270 billion in Taiwan, $763 billion in India, Indonesia, South Korea, Malaysia, and Thailand combined, and $948 billion in Japan.

These interventions have slowed the decline in the U.S. dollar that would have otherwise occurred. From July 20 2005 to February, 15, 2008, the U.S. dollar depreciated by 13.3 percent against the renminbi. However, this change reflects mostly a general decline in the nominal trade-weighted foreign exchange value of the U.S. dollar of 12.8 percent rather than a general appreciation in the foreign exchange value of the renminbi against other currencies (see Graph 3).

In contrast, major developed and developing economies outside of Asia have not accumulated excessive foreign exchange reserves (see Graph 2B). From July 20, 2005 to February 15, 2008, the renminbi has appreciated by 15.3 percent against the U.S. dollar. During the same period, however, the renminbi has appreciated by much less against the British pound (1.7 percent) and the Japanese yen (9.5 percent). The renminbi depreciated by 5.5 percent against the Canadian dollar, 5.4 percent against the euro, 4.1 percent against the Australian dollar, 3.0 percent against the Swiss franc, and 1.5 percent against the New Zealand dollar (see Graph 4).

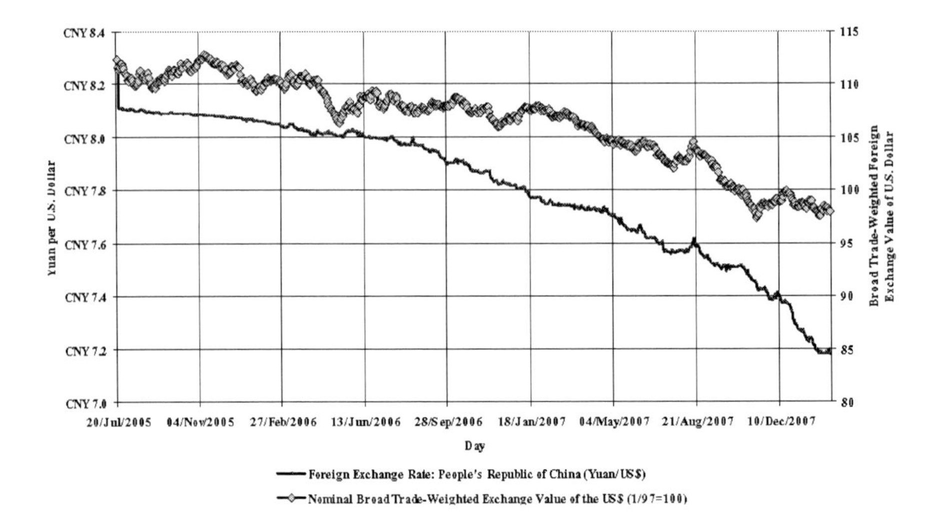

Graph 3. Change in Renminbi-U.S. Dollar Exchange Rate Reflects Broad Depreciation in Foreign Exchange Value of U.S. Dollar, Not Appreciation of Renminbi

Except for the Thai baht, the shadow interventions by central banks in other developing and newly industrializing economies in Asia have kept their currencies broadly in line with the renminbi. Between July 20, 2005 and February 15, 2008, the renminbi has appreciated by 5.2 percent against the Indian rupee and 4.4 percent against the Korean won, while the renminbi has depreciated against the Malaysian rinngit by 2.3 percent and the Singaporean dollar by 3.6 percent (see Graph 4).

There is wide agreement among economists that the renminbi is severely undervalued. Earlier this year, Morris Goldstein, a senior fellow at the Peterson Institute for International Economics, reported that the renminbi "is now grossly under-valued – on the order of 30 percent or more against an average of China's trading partners and 40 percent or more against the U.S. dollar."[5]

The PRC's intervention and the shadow interventions by other Asian economies have boosted the international demand for the U.S. dollar, increasing its foreign exchange value and exacerbating international imbalances. The PRC's current account surplus rose from 1.3 percent of GDP in 2001 to 9.0 percent of GDP in 2006. Global Insight forecasts that the PRC's current account surplus will be at least 9.1 percent of GDP for 2007. The U.S. current account deficit grew from 3.8 percent of GDP in 2001 to 6.2 percent of GDP in 2006, before falling to a seasonally adjusted annualized level of 5.1 percent in the third quarter of 2007.

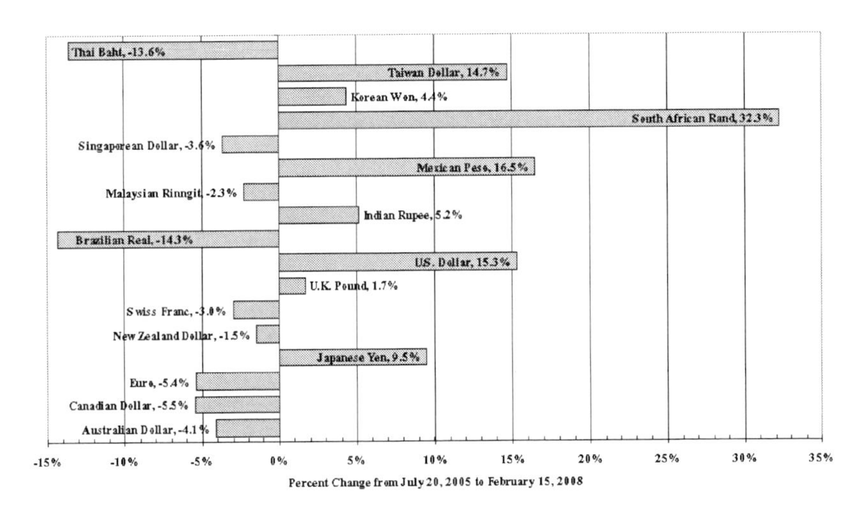

Graph 4. Changes in Exchange Rates of Major Developed, Major Developing, and other Asian Currencies against the Renminbi (July 20, 2005 to February 15, 2008)

The PBC and other Asian central banks have invested their foreign exchange reserves heavily in U.S. Treasury debt securities and U.S. Agency debt securities. As of September 30, 2007, 53 percent of all privately held U.S. Treasuries were owned by foreign residents.[6] About 70 percent of these foreign residents are, in fact, foreign government agencies, mainly central banks in east, southeast, and south Asia and sovereign wealth funds (SWFs) in oil-exporting countries in the Middle East.

This is a significant swing toward foreign ownership since December 31, 2000, when only 37 percent of all privately held U.S. Treasuries were owned by foreign residents. This swing is mainly attributable to a large increase in annual net purchases of U.S. securities by foreign governments from $28 billion (equal to 0.3 percent of GDP) in 2001 to $440 billion (equal to 3.3 percent of GDP) in 2006. Thus, the PBC's intervention and the shadow interventions by central banks in other Asian economies largely explain the spike in net purchases of U.S. securities by foreign governments during this period (see Graph 5).

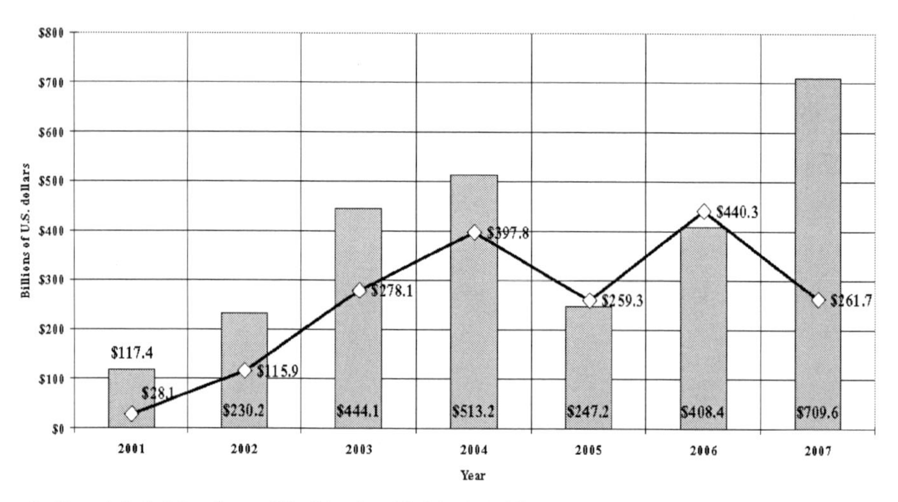

Graph 5. Annual Increase in Foreign Exchange Reserves and Change in Foreign Official Assets in the United States

IV. Economic Consequences

The PRC's exchange rate policy and its shadow policies in other Asian economies have enormous consequences for the United States and the rest of the world. These exchange rate manipulations have distorted prices and sent faulty signals to individuals and firms around the world.

A. Effects on China

- The PRC's exchange rate policy has reduced the real price of Chinese labor relative to labor in other countries. By lowering labor costs, the PRC encouraged a surge of inward direct investment by foreign multinational corporations (MNCs) in the labor-intensive manufacturing of low-tech goods and the final assembly of medium-tech consumer goods from imported parts. The rapid increase in both exports and imports by Chinese subsidiaries of foreign MNCs has driven the phenomenal growth of China's international trade.
- This exchange rate policy slowed the appreciation of the renminbi and the decline in the prices of imported goods and services in yuan terms. Consequently, Chinese households consume far fewer imported goods and services than they would without this intervention. Shadow exchange rate policies have also slowed the growth of domestic consumption of imported goods and services in other Asian economies.
- The PRC's exchange rate policy has effectively created a price ceiling known as the "China price" that severely limits the ability of manufacturers of labor-intensive goods in other countries to increase their prices and remain competitive.

B. Effects on the United States

- The China price has had disinflationary effects around the world.
- Because of the PRC's distortion of world prices, U.S. exports were lower and U.S. imports were higher than they would otherwise have been. Consequently, U.S. output and employment in the tradable

goods and services sector were lower than they would otherwise have been.

- The massive interventions by the PBC and central banks in other Asian economies have tended to reduce long-term interest rates in the United States both directly and indirectly since 2000. First, the PBC and other Asian central banks bid-down U.S. interest rates through their massive purchases of U.S. dollar-denominated debt securities. Second, the China price effect has slowed the increase in various price indices that are used to measure inflation. As a result, inflation and inflationary expectations have been contained. This has allowed the Federal Reserve and other central banks outside of Asia to pursue more accommodative monetary policies that have also helped to keep long-term interest rates low.
- By lowering long-term interest rates, the exchange rate policies of the PRC and other Asian economies deterred investment in the United States and other economies in parts of the tradable goods sector in which Chinese firms and Chinese subsidiaries of foreign MNCs are highly competitive and encouraged investment in non-tradable sectors, especially housing. Thus, these policies contributed to the inflation of a housing price bubble in the United States that peaked in 2006. As the bubble expanded, builders constructed too many new units, and too many households borrowed more than they could reasonably afford in order to buy homes. After the bubble burst, some of this residential investment has been revealed to be either overinvestment or malinvestment.
- The *Economist* reported that other developed countries outside of Asia had experienced a similar inflation in housing prices. "The S&P/Case-Shiller national index, the best gauge of American house prices, peaked last year after rising by 134 percent in the previous decade. France, Sweden and Denmark have all had booms of similar size. In Britain, Australia, Spain and Ireland, the ten-year increase ... has been even larger."[7] Thus, China's exchange rate policy and its shadow effect in other Asian economies may be contributing to significant distortions in investment decision-making worldwide. Since actual housing prices have risen much faster than housing price models based on the rates of household formation and real income growth would suggest, these increases in housing prices in developed countries outside of Asia may also be bubbles that will eventually

burst with similar growth-restraining effects to what the United States is now experiencing.

- During the bubble years, the speculative finance of housing became common. Prudent lending practices such as significant down-payments and the verification of a potential borrower's income, assets, and liabilities were swept aside. Marginal borrowers that might not be able to service their mortgage loans after teaser rates expired relied on ever rising housing prices to allow them to refinance their homes or sell them at a profit before higher rates kicked-in. These subprime residential mortgage loans were securitized into collateral debt obligations (CDOs) and sold to investors that did not understand the credit quality of the underlying loans and that instead relied on the ratings of credit agencies. After the bubble burst, many of these CDOs were unable to perform as their credit ratings implied, and their market value collapsed. Major commercial and investment banks were forced to write down the value of their CDO assets. The revulsion toward CDOs led to a wider re-evaluation of risk and re-pricing of credit. Despite significant injections of liquidity by the Federal Reserve since September 2007, the availability of credit for riskier transactions such as leveraged buyouts has contracted, and credit risk spreads have widened considerably. From July 2, 2007 to February 15, 2008, for example, the yield spread between Moody's seasoned 20-year grade Aaa (highest investment grade) corporate bonds and comparable Treasuries widened by 60 basis points, while the yield spread between Moody's seasoned 20-year grade Baa (the lowest investment grade) corporate bonds and comparable Treasuries expanded by 91 basis points (see Graph 6). Moreover, the yield spread between the Merrill Lynch index of "junk" corporate bonds (rated CCC by Standard and Poor's) and comparable Treasuries ballooned by 556 basis points. It has become more difficult and more costly for higher risk borrowers to obtain credit. This may reduce aggregate business investment in nonresidential structures, equipment and software and could make a recession more likely.

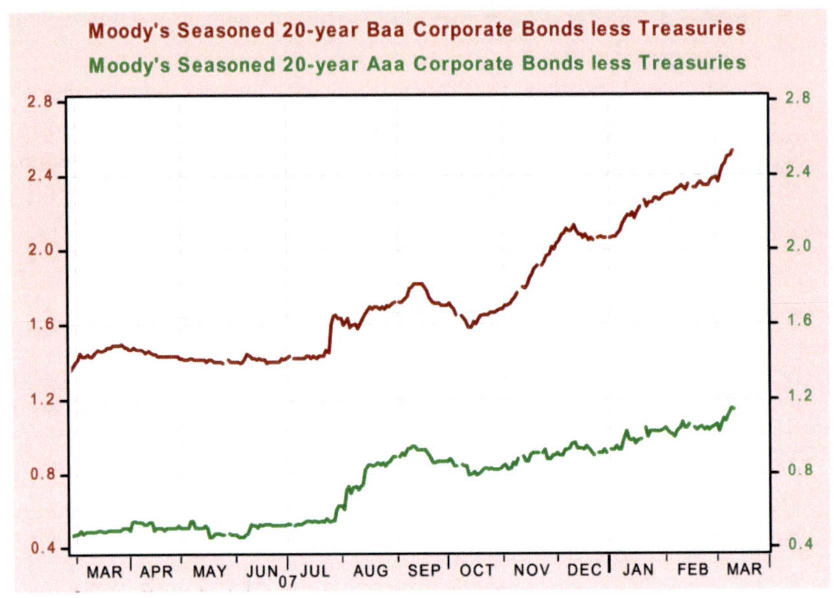

Source: Haver Analytics

Graph 6. Yield Spreads Widened after July 2, 2007

V. Dangers Ahead

The present imbalances in exchange rates and international accounts are unlikely to be sustainable.

- **The PBC's ability to sterilize its rapidly increasing foreign exchange** reserves may have reached its limit. Inflation is accelerating in China. Excess liquidity is inflating prices of assets as well as goods and services. In January 2007, consumer prices were up 7.1 percent from a year ago. Share prices on Chinese stock markets appear to be a bubble. From December 31, 2005 to January 14, 2008, share prices rose by 405 percent as measured by the Dow Jones Shanghai index before backing down by 15 percent through February 15, 2008. Domestic inflation **is now affecting China's export sector. After five** years of decline, the prices of Chinese manufactured exports are now increasing. The PBC has increased domestic interest rates six times in 2007 and expected to hike domestic interest rates further in 2008. In a desperate measure to curb swelling inflation, the Chinese Banking Regulatory Commission has imposed quotas limiting new loans at Chinese banks.

- Chinese leaders now face a politically uncomfortable choice between (1) maintaining current exchange rate policy to protect the vested interests in the current industrial structure at the cost of spiraling domestic inflation, or (2) allowing a rapid appreciation of the foreign exchange value of the renminbi to a market-determined level to cool domestic inflation and reduce international trade frictions.
- If Chinese leaders decide to allow the foreign exchange value of the renminbi to appreciate to a market-determined level, the dissipation of PBC's massive intervention in foreign exchange may cause the foreign exchange value of the U.S. dollar, which has already been decreasing, to drop further. Decisions by other Asian countries to allow their currencies to appreciate as well would amplify the depreciation of the foreign exchange value of the U.S. dollar.
- The disinflationary effects of the China price in other economies are likely to dissipate over the next few years through either renminbi appreciation or domestic inflation in China. To prevent domestic inflation from accelerating in the United States, the Federal Reserve may need to pursue a less accommodative monetary policy. As a result, longterm interest rates in the United States are likely to be higher.
- A lower foreign exchange value for the U.S. dollar should stimulate the tradable goods and services sector by increasing exports and reducing imports relative to baseline trends. Consequently, both the U.S. current account deficit and the U.S. capital and financial account surplus are likely to fall as a percent of GDP. However, higher long-term interest rates are also likely to prolong declines in housing prices and investment in residential construction and slow the liquidation of overinvestment and malinvestment in housing. Although beneficial to growth over the long term, a reduction in foreign exchange intervention is likely to dampen real GDP growth for several years.
- A major risk for the United States is that Asian central banks and SWFs in oil-exporting countries decide to reduce their exposure to fluctuations in the U.S. dollar by selling U.S. dollar-denominated assets and buying assets denominated in other currencies, probably euros. While some policymakers have hypothesized that the PBC or SWFs might try to liquidate a substantial portion of their U.S. dollar-

denominated assets in a political maneuver against the United States, this scenario is highly unlikely because such a "fire sale" would impose enormous financial losses on any country trying to liquidate its U.S. dollar-denominated assets at once. A plausible scenario is that the Asian central banks and SWFs may decide to allocate a smaller share of their portfolios to U.S. dollar- denominated assets over several years. Such a marginal portfolio reallocation could nevertheless place significant downward pressure on the foreign exchange value of the U.S. dollar for an extended period.

- A significant and sustained rally in the foreign exchange value of the U.S. dollar is unlikely to occur until market expectations for the future course of tax, regulatory, and trade policies after the 2008 election improve.

VI. Conclusion

The PRC's exchange rate policy and the shadow policies of other Asian governments have boosted the foreign exchange value of the U.S. dollar significantly above its market-determined level since 2000. These policies have distorted price signals around the world by holding down the prices of labor-intensive goods and lowering long-term interest rates. These distortions contributed to unsustainable imbalances in international accounts and to overinvestment and malinvestment, especially in housing in the United States.

If the PRC were to announce its intention to phase-out the PBC's interventions in foreign exchange markets over several years and to allow the renminbi to appreciate more rapidly until its foreign exchange value was determined solely by market forces at some fixed date in the future, the unwinding of these international imbalances and the liquidation of overinvestment and malinvestment would accelerate. Although this policy change would significantly improve the long-term growth prospects for China, the United States, and the rest of the world, it may slow real GDP growth in the United States for several years.

Robert P. O'Quinn
Senior Economist

APPENDIX: WHAT ARE INTERNATIONAL ACCOUNTS?

International accounts are a system of double-entry accounting that records all transactions between residents in a country and nonresidents during a time period, usually a year. In this system, there are two major accounts: (1) current account and (2) capital and financial account. This is subdivided into: (2a) capital account and (2b) financial account.

- (1) The current account records transactions in goods, services, income, and unilateral current transfers between residents and nonresidents.
- (2a) The capital account records capital transfers between residents and nonresidents, such as debt forgiveness and migrants' transfers, and acquisitions and disposals of non- produced, non-financial assets between residents and nonresidents.
- (2b) The financial account records transactions between residents and nonresidents resulting in changes in the level of international claims or liabilities, such as in deposits, loans, ownership of portfolio investment securities, and direct investment.

By definition, the (1) current account and the (2) capital and financial account should sum to zero for each country in the world. Thus, a current account surplus implies a capital and financial account deficit and vice versa. Any sum other than zero indicates errors by a country's statistical agency in recording and compiling international transaction data. To compare international account components both among countries and through time, economists normalize balance amounts with a country's contemporaneous gross domestic product (GDP). For example, the U.S. current account balance was 6.15 percent of GDP in 2006.

While many people falsely assume that any surplus must be good and any deficit must be bad, a current account surplus (or a surplus in any of its components including the trade balance) is not necessarily good for a country's economy nor is a current account deficit necessarily bad. Remember, a current account surplus requires a capital and financial account deficit. For example, a country whose economy is in a depression typically runs a current account surplus (because domestic demand for imports has collapsed) and a capital and financial account deficit (because residents and foreigners invest their funds in other countries).

End Notes

[1] In the United States, the dollar is the name of both the currency and the unit of account. In the People's Republic of China, the renminbi is the name of the currency, but yuan is the name of the unit of account. Thus, this study uses renminbi when referring to the Chinese currency as a concept and yuan when referring to an amount in terms of renminbi.

[2] U.S. Treasury debt securities are obligations of the U.S. government that carry the backing of the full faith and credit of the U.S. government. U.S. agency debt securities are obligations of U.S. government agencies or U.S. government-sponsored enterprises (GSEs) that do not carry the explicit backing of the full faith and credit of the U.S. government. However, bond market participants behave as if U.S. agency debt securities carry an implicit guarantee from the U.S. government. GSEs that regularly issue U.S. agency debt securities include the Federal National Mortgage Association (Fannie Mae), the Federal Home Loan Mortgage Corporation (Freddie Mac), and the Student Loan Marketing Association (Sallie Mae). Agencies that regularly issue U.S. agency debt securities include the Federal Farm Credit Banks, the Federal Home Loan Banks, and the Tennessee Valley Authority (TVA). As of December 31, 2007, U.S. Treasury debt securities outstanding were $4.5 17 trillion and U.S. agency debt securities outstanding were $8.836 trillion.

[3] For a discussion about the international account including definitions of the current account and the capital and financial account, please see the appendix.

[4] Overinvestment is investment that creates more assets than are needed to satisfy current demand for goods and services. Malinvestment is investment that creates the wrong kind of assets to satisfy current demand for goods and services. Overinvestment is generally less costly to liquidate than malinvestment. While overinvestment in assets can be liquidated by reducing new investment in such assets and by lowering the prices of such assets, malinvestment can be liquidated only by adapting existing assets to new uses often through additional investment. Thus, the losses to current asset owners are generally greater from malinvestment than from overinvestment. For example, a home builder may simply suspend new construction on single family detached houses until the inventory clears, while a developer that is constructing a condominium tower in a heavily overbuilt market may have to convert this project to a hotel at considerable expense.

[5] Morris Goldstein, "A (Lack of) Progress Report on China's Exchange Rate Policies," Presented to China Balance Sheet Conference (May 2007). Found *at:* http://www.chinabalance sheet.org/Documents/ExchangeRate.doc

[6] Gross federal debt is composed of federal debt in intra-governmental accounts and federal debt held by the public. Federal debt held by the public is composed of federal debt held by the Federal Reserve and privately held federal debt. By accounting convention, privately held federal debt includes all U.S. Treasury debt securities owned by international organizations and foreign residents. Foreign residents include foreign governments as well as foreign households and firms. See *Treasury Bulletin,* Table OFS-2 (November 20, 2007). Calculation of percentage is by author.

[7] Economic Focus: House Built on Sand, Economist (September 13, 2007). Found at: http://www. economist.com/finance/economicsfocus/displaystory.cfm?story_id=9804125

In: The Chinese Economy ISBN: 978-1-60876-937-7
Editors: Benjamin A. Tyler pp.115-122

Chapter 6

How Large is China's Economy? Does it Matter?

Wayne M. Morrison and Michael F. Martin

Summary

China's rapid economic growth since 1979 has transformed it into a major economic power. Over the past few years, many analysts have contended that China could soon overtake the United States to become the world's largest economy, based on estimates of China's economy on a "purchasing power parity" (PPP) basis, which attempts to factor in price differences across countries when estimating the size of a foreign economy in U.S. dollars. However, in December 2007, the World Bank issued a study that lowered its previous 2005 PPP estimate of the size of China's economy by 40%. If these new estimates are accurate, it will likely be many years before China's economy reaches U.S. levels. The new PPP data could also have an impact on U.S. and international perceptions over other aspects of China's economy, including its living standards, poverty levels, and government expenditures, such as on the military.

Measuring the Size of China's Economy

Since embarking on a road of free market reforms nearly three decades ago, China has been one of the world's fastest growing economies. The actual size of China's economy has been a subject of extensive debate among economists. China reports that its 2005 gross domestic product (GDP) was 18.4 trillion yuan.[1] Using average annual nominal exchange rates (at 8.2 yuan per dollar) yields $2.2 trillion, equal to less than one- fifth the size of the U.S. economy.[2] China's per capita GDP (a common measurement of living standards) in nominal dollars was $1,761, or 4.2% of U.S. levels. These data would indicate that China's economy and living standards in 2005 were vastly below U.S. levels. However, economists contend that these figures are very misleading. First, nominal exchange rates only reflect the price of currencies in international markets, which can vary greatly over time.[3] Secondly, some exchange rate mechanisms, such as between the dollar and the Chinese yuan, may be significantly distorted by foreign government intervention.[4] Finally, nominal GDP data fail to reflect differences in prices that exist across nations. Surveys indicate that prices in developing countries (such as China) are generally much lower than they are in developed countries (such as the United States and Japan), especially for non-traded goods and services. Thus, a measurement of a developing country's GDP expressed in nominal U.S. dollars will likely understate (often significantly) the actual level of goods and services that GDP can buy domestically.

Purchasing Power Parity and GDP Size

Economists have attempted to factor in national price differentials by using a purchasing power parity (PPP) measurement, which converts foreign currencies into a common currency (usually the U.S. dollar) on the basis of the actual purchasing power of those currencies (based on surveys of the prices of various goods and services) in each respective country. In other words, the PPP data attempt to determine how much local currency (yuan, for example) would be needed to purchase a comparable level of goods and services in the United States per U.S. dollar. This "PPP exchange rate" is then used to convert foreign economic data in national currencies into U.S. dollars.[5] One of the largest PPP projects in the world is the International Comparison Program (ICP), which is coordinated by the World Bank. The ICP collects price data on more than 1,000 goods and services in 146 countries and territories (and makes estimates of 39 others).[6]

The ICP's New PPP Estimates of China's GDP

Prior to December 2007, data from the ICP and various private economic forecasting firms all seemed to agree that China's economy, measured on a PPP basis, was close to $9 trillion in 2005, ranking it as the world's second-largest economy, after the United States. Based on these estimates, and projections of continued rapid economic growth, many analysts predicted that China's economy would surpass that of the United States within a few years.[7] Such projections helped fuel the growing debate over whether China posed an economic threat to the United States.[8] However, newly revised PPP data released by the World Bank in December 2007 purport to show that China's economy in 2005 was 40% smaller than previously estimated.[9] The ICP's previous 2005 PPP estimate of China's GDP (hereinafter referred to as *ICP 1*) at $8.8 trillion fell to $5.3 trillion (down by $3.3 trillion) under the ICP revision (hereinafter referred to as *ICP 2 revision*).[10] In addition, China's per capita GDP on a PPP basis dropped from $6,765 to $4,091 (see Table 1). The size of China's GDP relative to that of the United States fell from 71.3% under ICP 1 to 43.1% under *ICP 2 revision*, while per capita GDP relative to the United States dropped from 16.2% to 9.8%. Finally, the new revision decreased China's 2005 share of world GDP from 14.2% to 9.7% (the U.S. share rose from 20.5% to 22.5%).

According to the ICP, the major difference between the old and new estimates of China's economy is that the latter reflects, for the first time, the inclusion of recent price survey data provided by China.[11] Previously, the ICP estimated China's PPP data based on a 1986 comparative survey of prices in the United States and China and subsequent extrapolations of that data. *ICP 2 revision* significantly increased price level estimates within China's economy. The new data estimated that Chinese prices were on average 42% of U.S. levels (compared to 26% under the previous estimate), which is reflected in the change in the estimate of China's PPP exchange rate from 2.1 yuan to the dollar to 3.4. The revised data indicate it will likely take many more years than previously thought before China's GDP and living standards reach U.S. levels.[12]

Table 1. Comparison of Various Estimates of Chinese, U.S., and Japanese GDP on a PPP Basis: 2005

	China	United States	Japan
GDP values ($billions)			
Using nominal exchange rates	2,235	12,376	4,549
PPP basis (ICP 1)	8,819	12,376	4,013
PPP basis (ICP 2 revision)	5,333	12,376	3,870
Per Capita GDP ($)			
Using Nominal exchange rates	1,761	41,674	35,604
PPP basis (ICP 1)	6,765	41,674	31,401
PPP basis (ICP 2 revision)	4,091	41,674	30,290
Average annual exchange rates: local currency unit per dollar			
Nominal exchange rate	8.2	1.0	110.2
PPP rate (ICP 1)	2.1	1.0	125.1
PPP rate (ICP 2 revision)	3.4	1.0	129.6

Source: The World Bank, 2005 International Price Comparison Program, Preliminary Results, December 17, 2007.

Implications for China and for U.S.-China Economic Ties

Although China's access to assistance and loans from international development agencies may be unaltered by the ICP PPP revision, the data may directly or indirectly effect China's economic policies and its attitudes in international trade discussions. China may attempt to use the PPP revisions to boost its claim that it is a "poor" country and that, given its development needs and large numbers of people living in poverty, it should not be pressed to adopt economic reforms (such as changes to its currency policy) that could prove disruptive, or be expected to adopt policies that slow its economy, such as curtailing its energy use in response to international concerns over global climate change. As a recent article in *The Economist* put it, "China would probably be quite happy to see its GDP revised down, hoping that America might stop picking on a smaller, poorer economy."[13] In February 2008, the World Bank stated that the ICP's revised estimate of China's PPP exchange rate data would affect its estimates of poverty levels in China, based on the daily cost of basic needs (estimated at roughly $1 PPP) and household surveys on consumption. The Bank estimates that the new PPP revisions would raise the estimated poverty rate in China in 2004 from 10% to 13-17%, or an increase from 130 million to between 169 to 221 million. Thus, previous estimates may have underestimated the number of Chinese living in poverty by up to 91 million people.[14]

Regardless of how China seeks to present the overall status of its economic development, commentators are speculating on the possible implications of the smaller GDP estimate of China for its socio-economic situation and policies, including:

- *China's political stability may be weaker than previously thought* — In the past, dissatisfaction with China's economic condition has lead to public unrest (e.g. — Spring 1989). The rising number of protests and demonstrations over the last few years may reflect, in part, the dissatisfaction of China's poor with their lack of economic progress.[15] A 2005 article in *People's Daily* described China's growing income disparity as a "yellow alert" that could become a "red alert" in five years if the government failed to take proper actions.[16] A 2005 United Nations report stated that the income gap between the urban and rural areas was among the highest in the world and warned that this gap threatend social stability. The report urged China to take greater steps to improve conditions for the rural poor, and bolster education, health care, and the social security system.[17] The new PPP measurement may increase pressure within China to expand efforts to promote development in the rural areas where over 800 million people reside. According to a recent article in the *Atlantic Monthly*, some Chinese question why the government does not use its massive foreign exchange reserves to help alleviate poverty and respond to increasing income disparities across the country, rather than invest those funds overseas assets, such as in U.S. Treasuries.[18] Such a reallocation of China's investment portfolio might have repercussions for the U.S. economy.[19]

- *Lower prospects for democracy* — Prior to the release of the ICP revision report, some analysts had speculated that, once China reached a certain level of economic development and possessed a large and educated middle class, it would follow the examples of Taiwan and South Korea and begin to institute democratic reforms. The lower estimate of China's economy and living standards may dampen expectations in the West that China might soon move to adopt political reforms.[20]

- *Lower commitment to market reforms and trade liberalization* — In an effort to reduce income disparities and improve conditions for China's poor, there may be a return to some of the "command economy" methods of the past. The recent decision to impose strict price controls on basic food items and other household necessities might be seen as a temporary retreat from market reforms.

Finally, the ICP study may also alter how the U.S. government and the U.S. business community perceive China. The possible new view of China includes:

- *Reevaluation of the Chinese government's budget* — The PPP data may affect how U.S. policymakers evaluate China's spending levels on policies that affect U.S. policy. For example, the U.S. Defense Department's annual report on China's military spending includes conversions of China's budget data by the Chinese People's Liberation Army (PLA) from nominal U.S. dollars into PPP levels. The report estimated the PLA's 2003 budget in $30.6 billion in nominal dollars and $141 billion on a PPP basis.[21] The World Banks's PPP revision could significantly decrease this estimate and other measurements of Chinese military spending as well as various public spending programs.[22]

- *Smaller export market potential* — As a senior fellow at the Council on Foreign Relations wrote, "U.S. businesses and entrepreneurs hoping to crack the Chinese and Indian markets must come to terms with a middle class that is significantly smaller than thought. Companies with growth plans tied to the Indian and Chinese markets could face disappointing results."[23]

However, it is important to note the limitations of PPP estimates of GDP — and where and when they provide useful insight in economic analysis. Although the estimated size of China's economy decreases under the PPP revisions, other aspects on China's economy remain significantly large. For example, trade and international financial data are generally unaffected by the reduction in China's PPP GDP. It is estimated that in 2007, China overtook the United States to become the world's second-largest exporter (after the European Union).[24] Similarly, in 2006 China was the world's fifth-largest recipient of foreign direct investment, the largest steel producer, the second-largest consumer of oil, and by some accounts, the largest emitter of carbon dioxide (CO2). In addition, since 2006, China has been the world's largest holder of foreign exchange reserves ($1.5 trillion at the end of 2007).[25] Thus, despite the ICP results, China remains a major trade and economic power and a major potential global player in international finances and investment flows.

End Notes

[1] National Bureau of Statistics of China, *2006 China Statistical Yearbook.*

[2] China's currency is the renminbi, which is denominated in yuan.

[3] Thus, a country's GDP could rise significantly in one year, but if its currency depreciated sharply against the dollar during the same period, it could appear that the actual size of the economy decreased over the previous year when data is converted to dollars.

[4] The Chinese government intervenes heavily in exchange rate markets by buying dollars in order to limit the yuan's appreciation against the dollar. Many analysts contend that the yuan is significantly undervalued vis-a-vis the dollar. See CRS Report RL32 165, *China's Currency: Economic Issues and Options for U.S. Trade Policy* by Wayne M. Morrison and Marc Labonte.

[5] Some analysts contend that PPP exchange rates reflect the "true value" of what a country's exchange rate with the dollar would be if market forces prevailed and contend this can be used to calculate a currency's "undervaluation." However, others, including the World Bank, reject this theory.

[6] The ICP is an international program that conducts statistical price surveys of a comparable basket of goods and services across countries in order to estimate PPP values. The data is used by the World Bank, the International Monetary Fund, the United Nations, and other international agencies to develop programs and policy goals, such as poverty reduction.

[7] The Economist Intelligence Unit (EIU) and Global Insight both projected in November 2007 that China's economy on a PPP basis would overtake the United States by the year 2010.

[8] See CRS Report RL33604: *Is China a Threat to the U.S. Economy?*, by Craig K. Elwell, Marc Labonte, and Wayne M. Morrison.

[9] The World Bank, *2005 International Comparison Program, Preliminary Results*, December 17, 2007.

[10] The ICP made revisions to its estimates of GDP size for several other countries as well. India's estimated GDP fell by 40%, and the overall size of world GDP in PPP also dropped.

[11] Although the new PPP estimate for China is likely to be much more accurate than previous data that relied on an outdated survey, the data reflects price surveys over a limited part of China — 11 cities and surrounding rural areas — and it is not clear whether the PPP data accurately reflects average national price levels, especially since a large segment of the population lives in the countryside. Thus, the new China PPP estimate may somewhat overstate the national average of prices (which might increase the PPP exchange rate and GDP values), although the World Bank contends that this figure is not likely to exceed 5%.

[12] To illustrate, under the revision, China's GDP on a PPP basis, China could overtake U.S. GDP within roughly 13 years (from the 2005 baseline data), assuming average real GDP growth of 3% for the United States and 10% for China (both of which are optimistic projections), and no changes in price differentials between the two countries (which are unlikely).

[13] "A Less Fiery Dragon?" *The Economist*, November 29, 2007.

[14] World Bank, *China, Quarterly Update*, February 2008, p. 21.

[15] See CRS Report RL33416, *Social Unrest in China*, by Thomas Lum.

[16] "Party School Journal Warns Against China's Widening Income Gap," *People's Daily*, September 21, 2005.

[17] *China's Human Development Report 2005.*

[18] The Atlantic Monthly. *The $1.4 Trillion Question*, by James Fallows, January-February 2008.

[19] For an analysis of the possible repercussions of a reallocation of China's investments in U.S. Treasuries, see CRS Report RL34314, *China's Holdings of U.S. Securities: Implications for the U.S. Economy*, by Wayne M. Morrison and Marc Labonte.

[20] Conversely, some contend that a growing middle class may hamper democracy in China, especially if political reforms are seen as a threat to their own economic interests or to political instability. See, the Daily Yomiuri. *For China, Stability Comes Before Democracy*, January 13, 2008, p. 8.

[21] U.S. Department of Defense, *Annual Report to Congress, Military Power of the People's Republic of China, 2007*, May 2007, p. 26.

[22] The Department of Defense report does not describe how it arrived at its PPP estimate for China (or if that data was obtained from another source). The PPP exchange rate used by Defense was about 1.8 yuan per dollar, while ICP's rate was 2.0 (in 2003). If the new ICPs' revised PPP exchange rate (3 .4)were used, the estimated PLA budget on a PPP basis would fall to $85 billion.

[23] Walter Russell Mead, "The Great Fall of China," *Los Angeles Times*, December 30, 2007. While the level of Chinese consumer buying power may not be as large as once thought, the very size of China's population (1.3 billion) and its rapid economic growth make it a potentially huge market for U.S. goods and services. In 2007, China overtook Japan to become the third-largest destination for U.S. exports (after Canada and Mexico).

[24] Source: *The Economist Intelligence Unit (EIU) DataServices*. The EIU estimated U.S. and Chinese merchandise exports at $1,190 billion and $1,225 billion, respectively.

[25] China invests a large share of those reserves overseas, including in U.S. securities. See CRS Report RL34314, *China's Holdings of U.S. Securities: Implications for the U.S. Economy* by Wayne M. Morrison and Marc Labonte; and CRS Report RL34337, *China's Sovereign Wealth Fund*, by Michael F. Martin.

CHAPTER SOURCES

The following chapters have been previously published:

Chapter 1 – This is an edited, excerpted and augmented edition of a Joint Economic Committee Study, dated July 2006.

Chapter 2 – This is an edited, excerpted and augmented edition of a United States Congressional Research Service publication, Report Order Code Rs21625, dated June 17, 2009.

Chapter 3 – This is an edited, excerpted and augmented edition of a United States Congressional Research Service publication, Report Order Code RL33534, dated March 5, 2009.

Chapter 4 – This is an edited, excerpted and augmented edition of a Joint Economic Committee Research Report, #110-13, dated October 2007.

Chapter 5 – This is an edited, excerpted and augmented edition of a Joint Economic Committee Study, dated March 2008.

Chapter 6 – This is an edited, excerpted and augmented edition of a United States Congressional Research Service publication, Report Order Code RS22808, dated February 13, 2008.

INDEX

A

B

C

D

E

F

G

H

I

N

O

P

Q

R

S